SKY MY HUSBAND !
THE INTEGRALE

Ciel mon mari ! L'intégrale

Jean-Loup Chiflet

SKY MY HUSBAND !
THE INTEGRALE

Ciel mon mari ! L'intégrale

Dictionary of the running English
Dictionnaire de l'anglais courant

Dessins de Pascal Lebrun

Éditions Points

Cet ouvrage reprend l'essentiel des titres suivants :

Sky my husband ! Ciel mon mari !, © Hermé, 1985
Sky my kids ! Ciel mes enfants !, © Payot, 1991
Sky my old lady's !, Édition publicitaire hors commerce, © Bookmaker, 1992
Sky my husband II ! The Return, © Hermé, 1998

ISBN originaux (Première édition) :
ISBN 2-86665-020-4 pour *Sky my husband ! Ciel mon mari !*
ISBN 2-228-88435-9 pour *Sky my kids ! Ciel mes enfants !*
ISBN 2-86665-270-3 pour *Sky my husband II ! The Return*
ISBN 978-2-7578-1098-9

© Éditions Points, Novembre 2008, pour la présente édition.

Préface

Souvenez-vous, c'était la fin des années 50. La France, la vraie, la profonde, la « franchouillarde », celle du Piconbière et des congés payés à la « gueule d'atmosphère » se réveilla un beau matin de nouveau sous la botte ou plutôt, le chapeau melon de l'envahisseur : les FRANGLAIS avaient débarqué sur leurs yachts, envahissant notre douce France, détruisant tout sur leur passage à coups de bulldozers, violant à coups de sex-shops, embrochant la poule au pot à coups de barbecues, submergeant à coups de hot dogs les cafés du commerce qu'ils allèrent jusqu'à transformer en drugstores.

Monsieur Dupont-Durand était effondré. Il n'en croyait pas ses oreilles. Certes, il avait fini par s'habituer sans problème au chewing-gum des GI's libérateurs, ceux-là même qui dansaient le be-bop le week-end dans les dancings, mais là, ça devenait too much. Jamais la France n'avait été aussi humiliée par la perfide Albion depuis Jeanne d'Arc et Napoléon.

Heureusement, en 1964, la contre-attaque apparut sous la plume féroce d'Etiemble et son célèbre *Parlez-vous franglais ?*, terrible réquisitoire contre l'envahisseur. Il fut soutenu dans son courageux combat par l'inoubliable Fernand Reynaud et son *Restons français !* Grâce à ces farouches chevaliers, l'ennemi parut reculer mais en 1970 une nouvelle brèche apparut dans l'univers impitoyable du show-biz et du marketing où les meetings succédaient aux brainstormings, les box-offices aux hit-parades.

C'en était trop ! Le gouvernement français prit lui-même les choses en main, faisant voter une loi qui, en 1977, interdit l'usage des mots anglais dans le vocabulaire officiel, transformant pêle-mêle bulldozer en *bouteur*, marketing en *mercatique*, l'interview du speaker en *entretien de l'annonceur* et le container en *conteneur*.

Mais c'était trop tard ! La « franglisation » avait atteint son point de non-retour et personne ne pouvait plus empêcher monsieur Dupont-Durand de faire son jogging autour du parking. Même monsieur Robert, celui du dictionnaire, continuait de définir tranquillement dans son vénérable ouvrage une personne « sexy » comme « ayant du sex-appeal ». C'était un comble !

Mais était-ce donc si grave ? Ne valait-il pas mieux en rire ? Après tout, notre vaillant pays en avait vu d'autres et, comme chacun sait en France, si on n'a pas de pétrole et encore moins de vocabulaire, on a des idées et encore plus d'humour. Puisque l'anglais était là, on allait le cuisiner à la française et se le mitonner suivant une recette dont je vous livre le secret :

« Prendre un mot français, normal, au sens propre ou au sens figuré suivant la saison et les arrivages.

Chercher sa traduction littérale. Si l'on en trouve plusieurs, faire un choix arbitraire.

Introduire ce mot dans une locution courante (proverbe, expression officielle ou familière, citation, etc.). Si l'on aime les plats relevés, ne pas hésiter à parsemer d'argot.

Traduire la locution entière mot à mot.

Servir. »

Voilà, j'ai passé ces dernières années à élaborer et à tester patiemment, dans l'ombre de mon laboratoire, des recettes de cette nouvelle gastronomie. Celle qui me paraît la plus succulente a donné son titre à ce livre...

Quant aux autres, je vous laisse juge...

À la bonne vôtre ! (At the good yours !)

Jean-Loup Chiflet   John-Wolf Whistle

Avertissement   *warning*

Cher lecteur,

Avant de vous plonger à corps perdu (at lost body) dans ce fabuleux guide de l'anglais courant, apprenez à vous en servir et à en tirer un maximum pour être très vite à tu et à toi (to you and to you) avec vos interlocuteurs anglophones.

Ce guide se lit de haut en bas et de A à Z.

Vous trouverez ci-contre un schéma explicite qui devrait vous éclairer définitivement sur son utilisation.

Substantif français
Substantif anglais

CHOUETTE (*OWL*)

C'est super chouette
It is super owl

☞ *It is fantastic*

Expression française
(choisie au hasard
des recherches
linguistiques
de l'auteur) destinée
à illustrer la meilleure
utilisation
de ce substantif.

Traduction « sky »,
c'est-à-dire libre,
qualifiée par d'aucuns
d'anglais de cuisine.
À utiliser
dans les dîners en ville
et dans les cours
de récréation.

Traduction classique et même correcte,
recommandée par l'Université.
À utiliser dans les copies d'examens
et dans les pays anglo-saxons.

A

ABOIS (*BARKS*)

> Être aux abois
> **To be at the barks**
>
> ☞ *To be at your last gasp*

ABOYER (*TO BARK*)

> Quand les chiens aboient,
> la caravane passe
> **When the dogs bark,**
> **the caravan passes**
>
> ☞ *Let the world say what it will*

ACCIDENT (*ACCIDENT*)

> Ce mec-là, c'est un vrai accident
> **This guy is a true accident**
>
> ☞ *That guy is a real mess*

ACQUÉRIR (*TO PURCHASE*)

> Bien mal acquis ne profite jamais
> **Well bad purchased never profits**
>
> ☞ *Ill gotten ill spent*

AFFAIRE (BUSINESS)

Cette fille est une affaire
This girl is a business

☞ She's good in the sack

AIDER (TO HELP)

Aide toi, le ciel t'aidera
Help yourself, the sky will help you

☞ God helps those who help themselves

AILE (WING)

Avoir un coup dans l'aile
To have a blow in the wing

☞ To be tipsy

ALLER (TO GO)

Ça va fort
It goes strong

☞ Things are going well

16

Cette fille est une affaire
(*She's good in the sack*)

ALLUMER (TO SWITCH ON)

J'ai allumé une super nana
I have switched on a super girl

☞ *I came on to this beautiful girl*

Je me suis fait allumer à mon examen
**I made myself switched on
at my exam**

☞ *I failed my exam*

ÂME (SOUL)

L'âme sœur
The soul sister

☞ *A kindred spirit*

AMI (FRIEND)

Les amis de mes amis sont mes amis
**The friends of my friends
are my friends**

☞ *Love me, love my dog*

Faire ami-ami
To make friend-friend

☞ *To make friends with*

AMPOULE (BULB)

J'ai une ampoule au pied
I have a bulb at the foot

☞ *I have a blister on my foot*

ANDOUILLE (SAUSAGE)

Arrête de faire l'andouille !
Stop making the sausage !

☞ *Stop acting the prick !*

ÂNE (DONKEY)

Passer du coq à l'âne
To pass from cock to donkey

☞ *To change the subject*

ANGLAIS (ENGLISH)

Filer à l'anglaise
To spin at the English

☞ *To take French leave*

ANGUILLE (EEL)

Il y a anguille sous roche
There is eel under rock

☞ *There's a snake in the grass*

APPAREIL (CAMERA)

Dans le plus simple appareil
In the plainest camera

☞ *In your birthday suit*

ARRACHER (TO TEAR OUT)

Je m'arrache, vous me gonflez trop
**I tear me out,
since you are inflating me too much**

☞ *I'm leaving : you're so boring*

ARRÊT (STOP)

Il est sous le coup d'un mandat d'arrêt
**He is under the stroke
of a postal order of stop**

☞ *There is warrant out for his arrest*

ARTICHAUT (ARTICHOKE)

Elle a un cœur d'artichaut
She has a heart of artichoke

☞ *She is fickle hearted*

ASCENSEUR (ELEVATOR)

Il m'a renvoyé l'ascenseur
He sent me back the elevator

☞ He returned my favor

ASSIETTE (PLATE)

Ne pas être dans son assiette
Not to be in one's plate

☞ To be out of sorts

Un pique-assiette
A pick-plate

☞ A sponger

ASSURER (TO INSURE)

Ce type assure autant en maths
qu'avec les filles
**This guy insures as well
in mathematics as with the girls**

☞ This guy is as good at maths
as he is with girls

ATOME (*ATOM*)

Avoir des atomes crochus
avec quelqu'un
**To have hooked atoms
with someone**

☞ *To get on well together*

AVALER (*TO SWALLOW*)

Il avale des couleuvres
He swallows grass snakes

☞ *He is taken in*

AVOINE (*OAT*)

Mes vieux ne veulent pas
me donner d'avoine
My old don't want to give me oat

☞ *My parents don't want to give me
any money*

B

BABA (*RUM BABA*)

Il l'a eu dans le baba
He got it in the rum baba

☞ *He got it in the neck*

BAC (*FERRY*)

Passer son bac
To pass one's ferry

☞ *To graduate*

BAGUE (*RING*)

C'est un mauvais plan : elle est baguée
Bad map : she is ringed

☞ *It's a pity she's engaged*

BAGUETTE (*STICK*)

Mener à la baguette
To lead at the stick

☞ *To rule somebody with an iron hand*

BAHUT (CUPBOARD)

Je me suis fait virer du bahut
I have been turned out from the cupboard

☞ *I have been expelled from school*

BAIGNER (TO BATH)

Ça baigne dans l'huile
It bathes in the oil

☞ *Everything is fine*

BAIN (BATH)

Au bain-marie
At the bath-Mary

☞ *A water bath*

BALADER (TO GO FOR A WALK)

Il a les mains baladeuses
He has the hands going for a walk

☞ *He has wandering palms*

BALAI (BROOM)

Il est con comme un balai
He's stupid like a broom

☞ *He doesn't know his arse from his elbow*

BALANCER (TO SWING)

Balancer une vanne
To swing a sluice

☞ *To make a dig*

Être bien balancée
To be well swung

☞ *To be well built*

BALCON (BALCONY)

Il y a du monde au balcon
There is a lot of people on the balcony

☞ *She has a big bust*

BALEINE (WHALE)

Une baleine de parapluie
A whale of umbrella

☞ *An umbrella spoke*

BALISE (BEACON)

Je balise à mort en avion
I beacon to death in a plane

☞ *I'm terrified of flying*

BANDE (STRIP)

Faire bande à part
To make strip at share

☞ *To go it alone*

BANNIÈRE (BANNER)

C'est la croix et la bannière
It's the cross and the banner

☞ *It's the devil's own work*

BARAQUE (SHANTY)

Cette ordure m'a cassé la baraque
**This garbage has broken me
the shanty**

☞ *That bastard made me look like a fool*

BARBE (BEARD)

La barbe !
The beard !

☞ *What a bore !*

Au nez et à la barbe de quelqu'un
At the nose and at the beard of somebody

☞ *To be under your nose*

Rire dans sa barbe
To laugh in one's beard

☞ *To laugh up one's sleeve*

BASKET (BASKET)

Cette fille est barbante,
elle ne me lâche pas les baskets
**This girl is bearding,
she does not release me the baskets**

☞ *As well as being a pain,
that girl never leaves me alone*

BATEAU (BOAT)

Il m'a monté un bateau
He went me up a boat

☞ *He led me up the garden path*

Bâton (STICK)

Il met toujours des bâtons dans les roues
He always puts sticks in the wheels

☞ *He always puts a spanner in the works*

Il a une vie de bâton de chaise
He has a life of stick of chair

☞ *He has a wild way of living*

Parler à bâtons rompus
To speak at broken sticks

☞ *To talk about this and that*

Baver (TO SLAVER)

En baver des ronds de chapeau
To slaver rounds of hat

☞ *To have your tongue hanging out*

Bec (BEAK)

Clouer le bec
To nail the beak

☞ *To shut someone up*

BÊCHER (TO DIG)

Tu n'es qu'une sale bêcheuse
You are just a dirty digger

☞ *You're very haughty*

BERGE (BANK)

C'était une vieille peau
d'au moins trente berges
**It was an old skin of
at least thirty banks**

☞ *She was an old woman who was
at least thirty*

BERGÈRE (SHEPHERDESS)

Oh ! la jolie bergère Louis XVI !
**Oh ! the nice shepherdess Louis
the Sixteenth !**

☞ *Oh ! the beautiful easy chair !*

BESOIN (NEED)

Faire ses besoins
To do one's needs

☞ *To spend a penny*

31

BÊTE (BEAST)

Chercher la petite bête
To look for the little beast

☞ *To nit-pick*

BEURRE (BUTTER)

Être beurré
To be buttered

☞ *To be pickled*

On ne peut pas avoir le beurre
et l'argent du beurre
**You can't have the butter
and the money of the butter**

☞ *You can't have your cake and eat it*

Ils sont beurrés comme des Petits Lu
They are buttered like little Lu

☞ *They're plastered*

BIDON (JERRICAN)

Se bidonner
To jerrican one's self

☞ *To laugh*

32

Chercher la petite bête
(To nit-pick)

BILLE (MARBLE)

Il touche sa bille en littérature
He touches his marble in literature

☞ *He knows a thing or two about literature*

Question bouffe, elle touche pas sa bille
**Question puff, she does not touch
her marble**

☞ *She can't cook to save her life*

BLAIREAU (BADGER)

C'est pas le mauvais cheval
mais c'est un vrai blaireau
**He is not the bad horse
but he is a real badger**

☞ *He's not a bad sort but he's very stupid*

BLANC (WHITE)

Faire chou blanc
To make white cabbage

☞ *To fail completely*

Se regarder dans le blanc des yeux
**To look each other in the white
of the eyes**

☞ *To look someone straight in the face*

34

BLEU (BLUE)

N'y voir que du bleu
To see only blue

☞ *Not to smell a rat*

Attention ! Voilà les bleus !
Watch ! Here are the blues !

☞ *Watch out ! Here come the police !*

BOCAL (JAR)

C'est un agité du bocal
He is an agitated of the jar

☞ *He is crazy*

BŒUF (BEEF)

Un effet bœuf
A beef effect

☞ *An impressive effect*

On est pas des bœufs !
We are not beefs !

☞ *You should take us in consideration !*

Il a un bœuf sur la langue
He has a beef on the tongue

☞ *He has been paid to keep his mouth shut*

J'ai tapé le bœuf avec des super musicos
**I have smacked the beef
with super musicians**

☞ *I jammed with some great musicians*

BOIRE (TO DRINK)

Qui a bu boira
Who has drunk will drink
☞ *Once a thief, always a thief*

BOIS (WOOD)

Ne pas être de bois
Not to be of wood
☞ *To be only human*

BOÎTE (BOX)

Sortir en boîte de nuit
To go to box of night
☞ *To go to a night club*

36

BOL *(BOWL)*

J'en ai ras-le-bol de ces casse-bonbons
**I have it short the bowl
of these break-sweet**

☞ *I'm fed up with these morons*

BOMBE *(BOMB)*

Faire la bombe
To make the bomb

☞ *To paint the town red*

BON *(GOOD)*

Parfois c'est bonnard d'en tenir
une bonne
**Sometimes it's goodard
to hold a good one**

☞ *It's nice sometimes to get good and drunk*

Avoir quelqu'un à la bonne
To have somebody at the good

☞ *To be fond of someone*

37

BOND (JUMP)

Faire faux bond
To make wrong jump

☞ *To stand someone up*

BONHOMME (GENTLEMAN)

Aller son petit bonhomme de chemin
To go one's little gentleman of path

☞ *To tootle along*

BONJOUR (GOOD MORNING)

C'est simple comme bonjour
It's simple like good morning

☞ *It's as easy as pie*

T'as l'bonjour d'Alfred
**You have the good morning
from Alfred**

☞ *You are in trouble*

Il ne lit que des bédés...
Bonjour la culture !
**He only read designed bands...
Good morning the culture !**

☞ *« He only reads comics :
he's not very well read*

38

BONNET (*BONNET*)

C'est bonnet blanc et blanc bonnet
It's white bonnet and bonnet white

☞ *It is six of one and half a dozen
of the other*

BOSSE (*BUMP*)

Il a roulé sa bosse
He rolled his bump

☞ *He has been about*

BOTTE (*BOOT*)

J'ai rencontré une nana très chouette.
Elle me botte hyper
**I met a very owl girl.
She boots me hyper**

☞ *I met this great girl. I really like her*

BOUCHE (*MOUTH*)

Avoir la bouche en cœur
To have the mouth in heart

☞ *to simper*

La bouche en cul de poule
The mouth in ass of chicken

☞ *A pouting mouth*

BOUCHER (*TO CORK*)

En boucher un coin
To cork a corner

☞ *To knock someone sideways*

BOUCHON (*CORK*)

C'est plus fort que de jouer au bouchon
**It's stronger than playing
at the cork**

☞ *That's the limit*

BOUDIN (*BLACK PUDDING*)

Tiens, voilà du boudin
Hold it, here is some black pudding

☞ *(Famous words from the French
Legion anthem)*

40

BOUDIN (*SAUSAGE*)

Il a levé un de ces boudins, j'te dis pas !
**He has lifted one of these sausages,
I don't tell you !**

☞ *He was flirting with this hag !*

BOUFFI (*PUFFY*)

Tu l'as dit bouffi
You have said it puffy

☞ *You'd better believe it*

BOULE (*BALL*)

J'ai les boules avant les exams
I have the balls before the exams

☞ *I'm scared stiff before exams*

Perdre la boule
To loose the ball

☞ *To go nuts*

BOULETTE (MEAT BALL)

Il a fait une boulette
He made a meat ball

☞ *He made a blunder*

BOUQUET (BUNCH)

C'est le bouquet !
It is the bunch !

☞ *That takes the biscuit !*

BOURDON (HUMBLE-BEE)

Ça m'a filé le bourdon
It gave me the humble-bee

☞ *It gave me the blues*

BOURRE (FLOCK)

Ce mec est toujours à la bourre
This guy is always at the flock

☞ *That guy is always late*

J'ai tellement siroté que j'étais bourré
comme un coing
I have so much siruped
that I was flocked like a quince

☞ *I drank so much I was completely*
out of it

BOURREAU (*HANGMAN*)

Un bourreau des cœurs
A hangman of hearts

☞ *A ladykiller*

BOURRIQUE (*DONKEY*)

Elle me fait tourner en bourrique
She turns me into a donkey

☞ *She drives me up the wall*

BOURSE (*STOCK EXCHANGE*)

La bourse ou la vie !
The stock exchange or the life !

☞ *Your money or your life !*

BOUSCULER (TO JOSTLE)

Ça se bouscule au portillon
It jostles at the gate

☞ He can't get his words out, fast enough

BOUSSOLE (COMPASS)

Il a complètement perdu la boussole
He has completely lost the compass

☞ He went off his head

BOUTEILLE (BOTTLE)

Avoir de la bouteille
To have some bottle

☞ To be long in the tooth

BRANCHE (BRANCH)

Je suis plus branché jazz
que heavy metal
**I am more branched jazz
than heavy metal**

☞ I prefer jazz to heavy metal

BRANLER (TO SWING)

J'en ai rien à branler de ton blé
**« I have nothing to swing
of your corn »**

☞ *I'll have nothing to do with your money*

BRAS (ARM)

À bras-le-corps
At arm, the body

☞ *Arms round the waist*

Bras dessus, bras dessous
Arm on, arm under

☞ *Arm in arm*

BRIQUE (BRICKS)

Ça ne casse pas des briques
It doesn't break bricks

☞ *It is nothing to write home about*

BRISER (TO SMASH)

La politique ça me les brise
Politics it does smash them to me

☞ *Politics bore me to tears*

BROSSER (TO BRUSH)

Tu peux toujours te brosser
pour t'envoyer en l'air avec elle
You may always brush you,
to send yourself in the air with her

☞ *You don't stand a chance with her*

BÛCHE (LOG)

J'ai vachement bûché mon exam
et je me suis planté
I have cowly logged my exam
and I planted myself

☞ *I worked very hard for that exam*
and I failed it

BULLE *(BUBBLE)*

Quand je pense qu'il y en a qui ont assez
de pot pour coincer la bulle
**When I think that there are some
who have enough pot to wedge up
the bubble**

☞ *When I think there are those who are
lucky enough to have nothing to do*

Ça va chier des bulles
It's going to shit bubbles

☞ *It's going to hot up*

BUT *(GOAL)*

De but en blanc
From goal to white

☞ *At the drop of a hat*

C

ÇA (THAT)

Je ne pense qu'à ça
I only think of that

☞ *I have a dirty mind*

CABINET (TOILET)

Je connais son chef de cabinet
I know his chief of toilet

☞ *I know his private secretary*

CACAHUÈTE (PEANUT)

Avec les meufs j'assure pas une
cacahuète
**With the menwo I do not insure
a peanut**

☞ *I don't know how to deal with women*

CACHET (PILL)

Le cachet de la poste faisant foi
The pill of the mail making faith

☞ *Date as post mark*

Il court le cachet
He is running the pill

☞ *He chases after any sort of work*

CADAVRE (CORPSE)

Un cadavre ambulant
A travelling corpse

☞ *Death warmed up*

CADEAU (GIFT)

Ce n'est pas un cadeau
It is not a gift

☞ *She is a pain in my neck*

CAFARD (COCKROACH)

Avoir le cafard
To have the cockroach

☞ *To have the blues*

CAFÉ (COFFEE)

C'est fort de café
It is strong of coffee

☞ *It's over the top*

CAGEOT (CAGEOTTE)

Si tu voyais le cageot qu'il se farcit
**If you would see the cageotte
that he is stuffing himself**

☞ *You should see the witch
he's going out with*

CAILLER (TO CURDLE)

On se caille les miches !
One's curdle ones loaves !

☞ *It's freezing !*

CAME (CAM)

Ta came c'est vraiment de la daube
Your cam is real stew

☞ *Your drugs are lousy*

CAMION (LORRY)

Il est beau comme un camion
He is beautiful like a lorry

☞ *He is a real hunk*

CANARD *(DUCK)*

Faire un canard
To make a duck

☞ *To hit a wrong note*

Ça ne casse pas trois pattes à un canard
**It does not break three legs
to a duck**

☞ *It's not brilliant*

CANON *(GUN)*

On se boit un canon ?
Let's drink a gun ?

☞ *Do you fancy a jar ?*

Pendant les vacances j'ai rencontré
un mec canon
**During the holidays I have met
a gun guy**

☞ *I met this gorgeous guy
while I was on holidays*

Pendant les vacances, j'ai rencontré un mec canon
(*I met this gorgeous guy while I was on holidays*)

CAPOTE (OVERCOAT)

J'assure toujours avec mes capotes anglaises
I always insure with my English overcoats

☞ *To be on the safe side,
I always have French letters*

CAROTTE (CARROT)

Les carottes sont cuites
The carrots are cooked

☞ *There's no more hope*

CARTE (MAP)

Manger à la carte
To eat at the map

☞ *To eat à la carte*

CARTON (CARDBOARD)

Hier soir en boîte j'ai fait un carton
Last night in box I made a cardboard

☞ *I picked someone up last night*

56

Faire un carton
To make a cardboard

☞ *To make a good score*

CASQUE (*HELMET*)

C'est toujours moi qui casque !
It's always me who helmets !

☞ *I am the one who always has to fork out !*

CASSER (*TO BREAK*)

Ça ne casse pas des briques
It does not break bricks

☞ *Nothing to write home about*

Casser la croûte
To break the crust

☞ *To have a bite*

Aujourd'hui je suis cassé,
je suis sorti toute la nuit
**Today I am broken,
went out all over the night**

☞ *I'm a wreck today :
I was out all last night*

57

CASSEROLE (SAUCE PAN)

Je crois qu'elle va passer à la casserole
**I think she is going to pass
at the sauce pan**

☞ *I think she is going to get laid*

CATHOLIQUE (CATHOLIC)

Ne pas avoir l'air catholique
To look Anglican

☞ *To look shady*

CAUSER (TO SPEAK)

Causes toujours, tu m'intéresses
Speak always, you are interesting me

☞ *You can always talk, you don't impress me*

CHAGRIN (SORROW)

Une peau de chagrin
A skin of sorrow

☞ *Shagreen*

CHAIR (FLESH)

Bien en chair
Well in flesh

☞ *Plump*

CHAMPIGNON (MUSHROOM)

Appuyer sur le champignon
To press on the mushroom

☞ *To accelerate*

CHANDELLE (CANDLE)

C'est lui qui tient la chandelle
He is the one who holds the candle

☞ *He is the gooseberry*

CHAPEAU (HAT)

On lui a fait porter le chapeau
He had to wear the hat

☞ *He took the rap*

CHAR (TANK)

Arrête ton char, Ben Hur !
Stop your tank Ben Hur !

☞ *Pull the other one !*

CHASSE (HUNT)

Tirer la chasse
To pull the hunt

☞ *To flush*

CHAT (CAT)

J'appelle un chat un chat
I call a cat a cat

☞ *I call a spade a spade*

Donner sa langue au chat
To give one's tongue to the cat

☞ *To give up*

CHAUD (WARM)

Chaud devant
Warm before

☞ *Careful ! it's hot*

CHAUFFER (TO WARM)

Tu commences à me chauffer
avec tes trips cul
**You start to warm me
with your ass trips**

☞ *I'm sick of hearing about your screwing
around*

CHEMISE (SHIRT)

Je m'en fiche comme de ma première
chemise
I care as much as my first shirt

☞ *I don't give a fig of that*

Ils sont cul et chemise
They are ass and shirt

☞ *They are hand and glove*

CHER (EXPENSIVE)

Son cher et tendre
Her expensive and tender

☞ *Her beloved*

CHEVAL (HORSE)

Ce n'est pas le mauvais cheval
He is not the bad horse

☞ *He is not a bad guy*

CHEVEUX (HAIR)

Avoir mal aux cheveux
To have bad to the hair

☞ *To have a hangover*

CHEVILLE (ANKLE)

La cheville ouvrière
The worker ankle

☞ *The king pin*

CHIEN (DOG)

Avoir du chien
To have dog

☞ *To be sexy*

C'est le chienchien à sa mèmère
It's the dogdog at his mothermother

☞ *It's an old lady's little dog*

CHIER (TO SHIT)

> T'es chié ! Tu crains, merde !
> T'as sali mon new 501
> **You shit ! You fear shit !**
> **You have dirty my new 501**
>
> ☞ *You horrible little shit !*
> *You got my new jeans dirty*

CHOSE (THING)

> Je me sens tout chose
> **I feel all thing**
>
> ☞ *I feel under the weather*

CHOU (CABBAGE)

> C'est son chou-chou
> **He is her cabbage-cabbage**
>
> ☞ *He is her pet*

> Chou à la crème
> **Cabbage at the cream**
>
> ☞ *Cream puff*

> Je suis dans les choux
> **I am in the cabbages**
>
> ☞ *I am in a bind*

Il a fait ses choux gras
He made his fat cabbages

☞ *He capitalized on it*

CHOUETTE (OWL)

C'est super chouette
It is super owl

☞ *It is fantastic*

CIEL (SKY)

Être au septième ciel
To be at the seventh sky

☞ *To be on cloud nine*

CINQ (FIVE)

Un cinq à sept
A five to seven

☞ *A tryst*

CIRAGE (POLISH)

Je suis dans le cirage
I am in the polish

☞ *I'm out for the count*

64

CIRCULATION (*TRAFFIC*)

Avoir une mauvaise circulation
To have a bad traffic

☞ *To have bad blood circulation*

CIRER (*TO POLISH*)

Rien à cirer
Nothing to polish

☞ *Not to give a damn*

CLAIR (*CLEAR*)

C'est clair quoi !
It's clear what !

☞ *It's obvious*

CLASSE (*CLASS*)

Classieux l'appart. avec les poutres app.
**Classious the appart
with visible beams**

☞ *That's a classy flat with wooden beams*

CLASSE (CLASSROOM)

Avoir de la classe
To have some classroom

☞ *To be elegant*

CLIQUES (CLICKS)

Prendre ses cliques et ses claques
To take one's clicks and one's clacks

☞ *To clean up and clear out*

CLOCHE (BELL)

Déménager à la cloche de bois
To move at the wooden bell

☞ *To do a moonlight flit*

Il y a quelque chose qui cloche ?
Is there something which bell ?

☞ *What's the problem ?*

Se taper la cloche
To hit one's bell

☞ *To feed one's face*

CLOUER (TO NAIL)

Ça lui a cloué le bec
It nailed her beak down

☞ It shut her up

COCHON (PIG)

Copains comme cochons
Friends like pigs

☞ Inseparable friends

On n'a pas gardé les cochons ensemble
We have not kept the pigs together

☞ We are not that intimate yet

CŒUR (HEART)

Faire le joli cœur
To make the nice heart

☞ To court someone

67

COIN (*CORNER*)

Aller au petit coin
To go to the little corner

☞ *To go to the loo*

Sourire en coin
To smile in corner

☞ *To half smile*

COINCER (*TO WEDGE*)

J'adore coincer la bulle
I love wedging the bubble

☞ *I love taking forty winks*

COING (*QUINCE*)

Il est bourré comme un coing !
He is flocked like a quince !

☞ *He is completely out of it*

COLLET (*COLLAR*)

Collet monté
Collar mounted

☞ *Stiff necked*

68

COMBLE (ATTIC)

Être au comble de la joie
To be at the attic of the joy

☞ *To be overjoyed*

COMMODE (CHEST OF DRAWERS)

Ce n'est pas commode
It is not chest of drawers

☞ *It is not easy*

COMPTER (TO COUNT)

Compter pour du beurre
To count for butter

☞ *To count for nothing*

Son compte est bon
His count is good

☞ *He has had it*

CONFITURE (JAM)

C'est de la confiture pour les cochons
It is jam for the pigs

☞ *It's casting pearls before swine*

CONSEIL (*ADVICE*)

Un conseil d'administration
An advice of administration

☞ *A board of directors*

CONTRAVENTION (*TICKET*)

Faire sauter une contravention
To make a ticket jump

☞ *Using influence to avoid penalty*

COOL (*COOL*)

Mais où tu vas, toi ? Cool, cool Raoul
But where are you going ? Cool, cool Raoul

☞ *Calm down*

COQUELUCHE (*WOOPING COUGH*)

Il est la coqueluche du village
He is the wooping cough of the village

☞ *He is the idol of the village*

CORDE (*ROPE*)

Passer la corde au cou
To pass the rope at the neck

☞ *To have one's head in the noose*

CORNICHON (*GHERKIN*)

C'est le roi des cornichons !
He is the king of the gherkins !

☞ *He is the king of fools !*

COTON (*COTTON*)

Ça va être coton !
It's going to be cotton !

☞ *It's not going to be easy !*

COUCHE (LITTÉRAIRE) (*BED*)

Il en tient une couche
He is holding a bed

☞ *He is a cretin*

71

(SE) COUCHER (TO GO TO BED)

Une Marie couche-toi-là
A Mary go-to-bed

☞ *A tart*

COUP (BLOW)

Boire un petit coup
To drink a little blow

☞ *To have a drink*

Le coup de foudre
A blow of lightning

☞ *Love at first sight*

COUR (YARD)

Faire la cour
To make the yard

☞ *To court someone*

COURANT (CURRENT)

Tenez-moi au courant
Keep me at the current

☞ *Keep me informed*

COURIR *(TO RUN)*

Courir sur le haricot
To run on the bean

☞ *To get on someone's nerves*

COUSIN *(COUSIN)*

C'est un cousin à la mode de Bretagne
**He is a cousin in the fashion
of Brittany**

☞ *He is a distant cousin*

COUTEAU *(KNIFE)*

Il est arrivé avec sa bite et son couteau
He arrived with his dick and his knife

☞ *He arrived very relaxed*

CRACHER *(TO SPIT)*

Je suis allé à un super concert
où ça crachait des masses
**I went to a super concert
where it was spitting masses**

☞ *I went to a wonderful concert :
the music was hot*

CRAINDRE (*TO FEAR*)

Ça craint, je dirais même plus, c'est craignos
It fears and I would say even better, it's fearos

☞ *It's very dangerous*

CRAQUER (*TO CRACK*)

Cette meuf me fait craquer
This manwo makes me crack

☞ *I'm crazy about that woman*

CRASSE (*CRASS*)

Il m'a fait un plan crasse
He made me a map crass

☞ *He did me a bad turn*

CRASSE (*FILTH*)

Il m'a fait un plan crasse
He made me a filthy map

☞ *He did me a bad turn*

CRÈCHE (*CRIB*)

En ce moment, je crèche dans un squatt
These days I crib in a squat

☞ *Right now I'm living in a squat*

CRÉMAILLÈRE (*POT-HANGER*)

Pendre la crémaillère
To hang the pot-hanger

☞ *To give a house-warming party*

CRÈME (*CREAM*)

C'est la crème des crèmes
He is the cream of the creams

☞ *He is the very best*

CRÊPE (*PANCAKE*)

Crêper le chignon
To pancake the bun

☞ *To fight (among women)*

CREVER (BURST)

J'ai failli me faire crever dans le tromé
I falled to be burst
in the groundunder

☞ *I almost got stabbed in the metro*

CROCHET (HOOK)

Il vit entièrement à ses crochets
He lives completely at her hooks

☞ *He lives off on her*

CROIX (CROSS)

Croix de bois, croix de fer, si je mens
je vais en enfer
Wooden cross, iron cross, if I lie
I go to hell

☞ *Cross my heart and hope to die*

CROQUER (TO CRUNCH)

Mignonne à croquer
Beautiful to crunch

☞ *Pretty as a picture*

CROÛTE (*CRUST*)

Casser la croûte
To break the crust

☞ *To have a bite*

CUILLÈRE (*SPOON*)

Il n'y va pas avec le dos de la cuillère
**He doesn't go with the back
of the spoon**

☞ *He makes no bones about it*

J'ai fini en deux coups de cuillère à pot
**I finished in two blows of spoon
to pot**

☞ *I finished in two shakes of a lamb's tail*

Il est à ramasser à la petite cuillère
**He is to be picked up
with a little spoon**

☞ *He is wiped out*

CUIRE (TO COOK)

C'est du tout cuit
It is all cooked

☞ *It's in the bag*

Être dur à cuire
To be hard to cook

☞ *To put up a strong resistance*

Les carottes sont cuites
The carrots are cooked

☞ *The die is cast*

Je suis cuit
I am cooked

☞ *It's all up for me*

Hier soir, je me suis pris une sacrée cuite
Last night I got a holy cook

☞ *Last night I got drunk out of my skull*

CUISSE (THIGH)

Avoir la cuisse légère
To have the light thigh

☞ *To be promiscuous*

CUL (ASS)

Cul de sac
Ass of bag

☞ *Cul de sac*

Bouche en cul de poule
Mouth in ass of chicken

☞ *Pursed lips*

Faire cul sec
To do dry ass

☞ *To down in one*

Être comme cul et chemise
To be like ass and shirt

☞ *To be best friends*

La digue du cul
The pier of the ass

☞ *Words of a famous French popular song*

La peau du cul
The skin of the ass

☞ *Very expensive*

D

DALLE *(PAVING STONE)*

On crève la dalle dans cette soirée
**One burst the paving stone
in this party**

☞ *There's nothing to eat at this party*

DÉCHIRER *(TO TEAR)*

Après ma nuit d'enfer,
je suis complètement déchiré
**After my night of hell which,
I am completely torn**

☞ *After my wild night, I'm a total wreck*

DÉFAUT *(DEFECT)*

Faire défaut
To do defect

☞ *To lack*

DÉFONCER *(TO KNOCK DOWN)*

Elles sont fortes ces tiges,
elles me défoncent
**They are strong these stems,
they are knocking me down**

☞ *These cigarettes are so strong,
I'm having trouble smoking them*

DÉGÂT (DAMAGE)

Un verre, ça va, deux verres,
bonjour les dégâts
**One glass, it goes, two glasses,
good morning the damages**

☞ *One glass is OK, but after,
things start going downhill*

DÉLIRE (DELIRIOUS)

C'est pas vrai, tu délires ?
It is not true, you are delirious ?

☞ *It can't be, you're joking*

DEMAIN (TOMORROW)

Ce n'est pas demain la veille
It is not tomorrow the day before

☞ *Not to be about to do something*

DEMEURE (MANSION)

Mettre en demeure
To put in mansion

☞ *To oblige*

DÉMON (DEVIL)

Le démon de midi
The devil of noon

☞ The midlife crisis

DENT (TOOTH)

Avoir une dent contre quelqu'un
To have a tooth opposite somebody

☞ To have something against somebody

Quand les poules auront des dents !
When the hens will have teeth !

☞ When the devil is blind !

DESCENDRE (TO GO DOWN)

Avoir une bonne descente
To have a good going down

☞ To be able to hold one's drink

DESTROY (TO DESTROY)

Il est complètement destroy, ce mec
He is completely destroyed this guy

☞ That guy is out of his mind

DEVANT (*IN FRONT*)

> Gros Jean comme devant
> **Big John like in front**
>
> ☞ *Like a booby*

DIRE (*TO SAY*)

> Le qu'en-dira-t-on
> **The what-will-one-say**
>
> ☞ *What will the neighbours say*

DIRE (*TO TELL*)

> Il est arrivé avec une tire ! J'te dis pas !
> **He came with a pull ! I don't tell you !**
>
> ☞ *He arrived in this super car, I'm telling you !*

DOIGT (*FINGER*)

> Tu te mets le doigt dans l'œil
> **You put your finger in the eye**
>
> ☞ *You are completely wrong*

DONNER (*TO GIVE*)

> C'est donnant donnant
> **It's giving giving**
>
> ☞ *You scratch my back, I'll scratch yours*

Quelle douche écossaise
(*What a disappointment!*)

DOUCHE (*SHOWER*)

> Quelle douche écossaise !
> **What a scottish shower !**
>
> ☞ *What a disappointment !*

DRAGÉE (*SUGARED ALMOND*)

> Il lui tient la dragée haute
> **He is holding him high up**
> **the sugared almond**
>
> ☞ *He looks down on him*

DRAP (*BED SHEET*)

> Être dans de beaux draps
> **To be in nice bed sheets**
>
> ☞ *To be in a fix*

DUR (*HARD*)

> Dur dur !
> **Hard hard !**
>
> ☞ *It's not easy*

E

EAU (*WATER*)

J'en ai l'eau à la bouche
I have the water at the mouth

☞ *It makes my mouth watering*

ÉCHAPPER (*TO ESCAPE*)

Il l'a échappé belle
He escaped it beautiful

☞ *He had a narrow escape*

ÉCORCHER (*TO FLAY*)

Ça t'écorcherait la gueule d'être poli ?
**Would it flay your muzzle
to be polite ?**

☞ *Couldn't you be a bit more civil ?*

EMBALLER (*TO WRAP*)

Emballez, c'est pesé !
Wrap it up, it's weighed !

☞ *That's does the job !*

EMBROUILLER (TO TANGLE)

Je me suis embrouillé avec des taggeurs
I tangled myself with taggers

☞ *I had a fight with some taggers*

EMMÊLER (TO MIX UP)

Je me suis emmêlé les pinceaux
I've mixed up my brushes

☞ *I tripped myself up*

EMPRUNTER (TO BORROW)

Avoir un air emprunté
To have a borrowed air

☞ *To look uncomfortable*

ENFANT (CHILD)

C'est un enfant de la balle
He is a child of the ball

☞ *He is a child of the theater*

MES HOMMAGES

BONJOUR MADAME

AVEC PLAISIR

MERCI MONSIEUR

APRÈS VOUS

Ça t'écorcherait la gueule d'être poli ?
(Couldn't you be a bit more civil ?)

ENFER (HELL)

Putain ! J'ai vu une meule d'enfer
Prostitute ! I have seen a grinding wheel of hell

☞ *Christ ! I saw this incredible motorbike*

ENFLER (TO SWELL)

T'es qu'une enflure
You are just a swelling

☞ *You poor creep*

ENREGISTRER (TO RECORD)

Enregistrer ses bagages
To record one's luggage

☞ *To check in baggage*

ENTENDRE (TO HEAR)

À bon entendeur, salut !
At good hearer, goodbye !

☞ *Once and for all, goodbye !*

ENTERRER (TO BURY)

Enterrer sa vie de garçon
To bury one's boy's life

☞ *To throw a stag party*

ENVOYER (TO SEND)

S'envoyer en l'air
To send oneself in the air

☞ *To have it off*

Se faire envoyer sur les roses
To be sent on the roses

☞ *To be sent about one's business*

ÉPINARD (SPINACH)

Ça va mettre du beurre dans les épinards
It will put butter in the spinachs

☞ *It's going to ease the situation*

ÉPINGLE (*PIN*)

Tiré à quatre épingles
Drawn at four pins

☞ *Dressed up like a dog's dinner*

Il a tiré son épingle du jeu
He pulled his pin from the game

☞ *He played the game skillfully*

ÉPONGE (*SPONGE*)

Je passe l'éponge
I pass the sponge

☞ *I'll forget all about it*

ESCALIER (*STAIRCASE*)

Il a l'esprit de l'escalier
He has the spirit of the staircase

☞ *He never thinks of an answer until it is too late*

ESSUYER (*TO WIPE*)

Essuyer un refus
To wipe a refusal

☞ *To meet with a refusal*

ESTOMAC (STOMACH)

Avoir l'estomac dans les talons
To have one's stomach in one's heels

☞ *To be starving*

ÉTOILE (STAR)

J'adore coucher à la belle étoile
I love to sleep at the nice star

☞ *I love sleeping in the open air*

ÉTONNER (TO ASTONISH)

Tu m'étonnes, John !
You astonish me, John !

☞ *I agree with you*

ÉTRIER (STIRRUP)

Le coup de l'étrier
The hit of the stirrup

☞ *One for the road*

ÉVENTAIL (FAN)

Elle a les doigts de pied en éventail
She has the toes in fan

☞ *She is in clover*

EXPLOSER (TO EXPLODE)

Je suis explosé de rire
I am exploded of laugh

☞ *I burst out laughing*

F

FACTURE (INVOICE)

Être de bonne facture
To be of good invoice

☞ *To be of good quality*

FAGOT (FIREWOOD)

Voici une bonne bouteille de derrière
les fagots
**Here is a good bottle from behind
the firewoods**

☞ *Here is a bottle of the best*

FAIBLE (WEAK)

Avoir un faible pour quelqu'un
To have a weak for somebody

☞ *To have a crush on someone*

FAÏENCE (EARTHENWARE)

Se regarder en chiens de faïence
**To look at each other in dogs
of earthenware**

☞ *To glare at one another*

FAIRE (*TO MAKE*)

Fait comme un rat
Made like a rat

☞ *To be cornered*

Faire le beau
To make the nice

☞ *To beg*

C'est pas fait pour les chiens !
It's not made for the dogs !

☞ *It's there to be used !*

FARCE (*JOKE*)

Il est le dindon de la farce
He is the turkey of the joke

☞ *He is the butt of the joke*

FARCIR (*TO STUFF*)

Mes parents, il faut se les farcir !
My parents, you have to stuff them !

☞ *You have to be able to put up with my parents*

102

FARINE (FLOUR)

Je me suis fait rouler dans la farine
I was rolled in the flour

☞ I was had

FATIGUER (TO TIRE)

Je vais fatiguer la salade
I am going to tire the salad

☞ I am going to toss the salad

FAUTEUIL (ARMCHAIR)

Il est arrivé dans un fauteuil
He arrived in an armchair

☞ He won hands down

FAUX (WRONG)

Faux cul !
Wrong ass !

☞ Two faced prick !

Sur ce plan-là, t'as tout faux
**On this map you have
everything wrong**

☞ As regards that, you're completely wrong

FER (*IRON*)

C'est un véritable bras de fer
It's a real arm of iron

☞ *It's a wrestling match*

FESSE (*BUTTOCK*)

Un fesse-Mathieu
A buttock-Matthew

☞ *A skinflint*

Ça coûte la peau des fesses
It costs the skin of the buttocks

☞ *It costs an arm and a leg*

FEU (*FIRE*)

Feu, le roi votre père
Fire, the king your father

☞ *The late king your father*

FEUILLE (*LEAF*)

Dur de la feuille
Hard of the leaf

☞ *Hard of hearing*

104

FIER (*PROUD*)

Fier-à-bras
Proud-to-arm

☞ *A wise guy*

Il me doit une fière chandelle
He owes me a proud candle

☞ *He is deeply indebted to me*

FIL (*THREAD*)

Aller au fil de l'eau
To go at the thread of water

☞ *To drift*

Passer au fil de l'épée
To pass at the thread of the sword

☞ *To run someone through with a sword*

Un coup de fil
A knock of thread

☞ *A phone call*

Il n'a pas inventé le fil
à couper le beurre
**He did not invent the thread
to cut the butter**

☞ *He'll never set the Thames on fire*

FILER *(TO THREAD)*

> Filer le parfait amour
> **To thread the perfect love**
>
> ☞ *To live an idyllic love*

FILET *(NET)*

> Un faux-filet
> **A wrong net**
>
> ☞ *A type of steak*

FILLE *(DAUGHTER)*

> Je descends à « Filles du Calvaire »
> **I go down at « Daughters
> of Calvary »**
>
> ☞ *I get off at the metro « Filles du Calvaire »*

FINIR *(TO FINISH)*

> Finir en beauté
> **To finish in beauty**
>
> ☞ *To end in glory*

FLAMBER (TO FLAME)

Les Reebok, c'est vraiment de la flambe
The Reeboks, it is really flame

☞ *Wearing Reeboks is just showing off*

FLAN (CUSTARD)

Il en est resté comme deux ronds de flan
**He stayed like two rounds
of custard**

☞ *You could have knocked him down
with a feather*

Elle m'a fait un flan et j'ai poireauté
deux heures
**She made me a custard and I leeked
two hours**

☞ *She lied to me and I waited for her
for two hours*

FLASHER (FLASH)

J'ai complètement flashé sur cette fille
I completely flashed on this girl

☞ *I'm really interested in that girl*

FLEUR (FLOWER)

Elle est « fleur bleue »
She is « blue flower »

☞ A prude

Elle est dans la fleur de l'âge
She is in the flower of the age

☞ She is in the prime of life

FLIPPER (TO FLIP)

Pour mon bac, je flippe total
For my ferry, I am flipping total

☞ I'm terrified about my graduation exam

FOIE (LIVER)

Avoir les foies
To have the livers

☞ To be scared stiff

FOIN (HAY)

J'ai fait un foin terrible
I made a terrible hay

☞ I kicked up

108

FOIRE (FAIR)

Il y a une bande d'enfoirés
que je ne peux pas encaisser
**There is a band of enfaired
that I cannot cash**

☞ *There's a crowd of shits I can't stand*

Faire la foire
To make the fair

☞ *To party*

FOND (BOTTOM)

Aller à fond de train
To go at bottom of train

☞ *To go flat out*

FONTAINE (FOUNTAIN)

Ne dis pas « Fontaine, je ne boirai pas
de ton eau »
**Don't say « Fountain, I will not
drink your water »**

☞ *Never say never*

109

FORGER (TO FORGE)

C'est en forgeant qu'on devient forgeron
It is in forging that you become blacksmith

☞ *Practice makes perfect*

FOUETTER (TO WHIP)

Il n'y a pas de quoi fouetter un chat
There is nothing to whip a cat

☞ *There is nothing to make a fuss about*

FOUR (OVEN)

Faire un four
To make an oven

☞ *To fall flat*

FOYER (HOME)

Il porte des verres à double foyer
He wears glasses at double home

☞ *He wears bifocal lenses*

Les frais généraux
(*The overheads*)

FRAIS (COOL)

Aux frais de la Princesse
At the cool of the Princess
☞ At Her Majesty's expense

Faire les frais de la conversation
To do the cool of the conversation
☞ To lead the conversation

Les frais généraux
The general cool
☞ The overheads

FRAIS (FRESH)

Se mettre en frais
To put oneself in fresh
☞ To go to great expenses

FRAISE (STRAWBERRY)

Sucrer les fraises
To sugar the strawberries
☞ To be old and doddery

Ramène pas ta fraise, Desbois
Don't bring back your strawberry, Desbois
☞ Don't show off, Desbois

FRANC (*FRANK*)

Pas franc du collier
Not frank of the collar

☞ *Fishy*

FRIRE (*TO FRY,*

J'ai failli me fritter avec des mecs
qui me prenaient le crâne
**I almost fried myself with guys
who where taking me the skull**

☞ *I almost fought with some guys who were
getting on my case*

FRISER (*TO CURL*)

Ça frise le ridicule
It's curling the ridiculous

☞ *It borders the ridiculous*

FROID (*COLD*)

Un froid de canard
A cold of duck

☞ *Brass monkey weather*

Être en froid
To be in cold

☞ *To be on the outs with someone*

FROMAGE (CHEESE)

N'en fais pas tout un fromage
Don't make a cheese of it

☞ *Don't make a big deal of it*

Entre la poire et le fromage
Between the pear and the cheese

☞ *Over coffee*

FUMER (TO SMOKE)

Fume, c'est du belge !
Smoke, it's Belgian !

☞ *Enjoy !*

FUSIL (GUN)

Elle dort en chien de fusil
She sleeps in dog of gun

☞ *She sleeps like a hammer*

G

GAFFE (HOOK)

Faire une gaffe
To do a hook

☞ To make a blunder

T'as intérêt à faire gaffe !
You have interest to make hook !

☞ You'd better look out !

GAGNER (TO WIN)

Un gagne-pain
A win-bread

☞ A job which pays the bills

GALÈRE (SLAVE SHIP)

Il a toujours des plans galères
He has always slave ship maps

☞ He always makes a mess of things

GAMELLE (KETTLE)

Ramasser une gamelle
To pick up a kettle

☞ To fail

117

GARDER (TO KEEP)

Garde-à-vous !
Keep to you !

☞ *Attention !*

Garder un chien de sa chienne
To keep a dog from one's bitch

☞ *To have it in for someone*

GARE (STATION)

Sans crier gare
Without shouting station

☞ *Without warning*

GAUCHE (LEFT)

Passer l'arme à gauche
To pass the weapon to the left

☞ *To kick the bucket*

GAULE (*STICK*)

J'te raconte pas comment
qu'elle est gaulée, la meuf
**I don't tell you how she is sticked
the manwo**

☞ *I can't tell you how beautiful
that woman is*

GAVER (*TO CRAM*)

Votre plan boîte, franchement,
ça me gave
Your box map, frankly, it crams me

☞ *I don't want to go out to a night club
with you*

GAZ (*GAS*)

Il y a de l'eau dans le gaz
There is water in the gas

☞ *There is a problem*

Vite fait sur le gaz
Quick made on the gas

☞ *Chop chop*

GÉANT (GIANT)

C'est géant ce qu'on a goupillé
pour les vacances
**It is giant, what we pinned
for the holidays**

☞ *We've planned something marvellous
for our holidays*

GENOU (KNEE)

Faire du genou
To make knee

☞ *To play footsie*

GENRE (KIND)

Genre, t'as eu ton bac ?
Kind, you got your ferry ?

☞ *You're certain you got your graduation
exam ?*

Bon chic bon genre
Good knack good kind

☞ *Preppy*

GERBE (SHEAF)

J'ai la gerbe tellement je mouille
I have the sheaf so much I wet

☞ *I'm so scared I want to throw up*

GLACE (MIRROR)

Veux-tu une glace à la fraise ?
Do you want a strawberry mirror ?

☞ *Do you want a strawberry ice cream ?*

GLAND (ACORN)

Arrête de glander
Stop to acorn

☞ *Stop idling*

GNOME (GNOME)

Ton beau-frère, c'est un vrai gnome
Your nice brother is a true gnome

☞ *Your brother-in-law is a fool*

121

GONFLER (TO INFLATE)

Il est vachement gonflé
He is cowly inflated

☞ *He has got a cheek*

Tu me gonfles
You are inflating me

☞ *You're annoying me*

GORGE (THROAT)

Faire des gorges chaudes
To do warm throats

☞ *To keep people talking*

GRAPPE (CLUSTER)

Lache-moi la grappe !
Leave me the cluster !

☞ *Leave it out !*

GRENOUILLE (FROG)

C'est une grenouille de bénitier
She is frog of stoup

☞ *She is a church mouse*

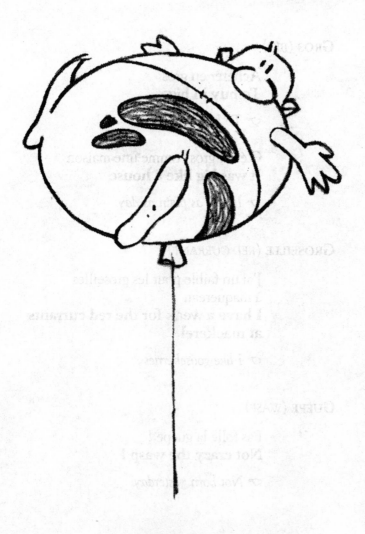

Il est vachement gonflé
(He has got a cheek)

GROS (BIG)

Acheter en gros
To buy in big

☞ To buy wholesale

C'était gros comme une maison
It was big like a house

☞ It was as plain as day

GROSEILLE (RED CURRANT)

J'ai un faible pour les groseilles
à maquereau
**I have a weak for the red currants
at mackerel**

☞ I like gooseberries

GUÊPE (WASP)

Pas folle la guêpe !
Not crazy the wasp !

☞ Not born yesterday

GUERRE (WAR)

De guerre lasse
From tired war

☞ *Finally*

C'est de bonne guerre
It is of good war

☞ *Fair's fair*

À la guerre comme à la guerre
At the war like at the war

☞ *We shall have to rough it, that's all*

Ce n'est pas un foudre de guerre
He is not a lightning of war

☞ *He is not outstanding*

GUEULE (MOUTH)

J'ai la gueule de bois
I have the mouth of wood

☞ *I have a hangover*

H

HAINE (*HATE*)

C'est la haine ! On m'a taxé mon Perf
**It is the hate ! One has taxed
my Perf**

☞ *It's awful ! Someone has stolen
my leather bomber jacket*

HALEINE (*BREATH*)

De longue haleine
Of long breath

☞ *Long term*

HALLUCINER (*TO HALLUCINATE*)

Tu hallucines, ou quoi ?
You hallucinate or what ?

☞ *Are you nuts or what ?*

HANNETON (*BEETLE*)

Pas piqué des hannetons !
Not picked of the beetles !

☞ *A helluva...*

129

HARICOTS (BEANS)

La fin des haricots
The end of the beans

☞ *The last straw*

HAUT (HIGH)

Tenir le haut du pavé
To hold the high of the pavement

☞ *To lord it*

HERBE (GRASS)

Il m'a coupé l'herbe sous le pied
He cut the grass under my foot

☞ *He took the words out of my mouth*

HEURE (HOUR)

À la bonne heure !
At the good hour !

☞ *Well done !*

Ça baigne dans l'huile
(*Everything is going smoothly*)

HIRONDELLE (SWALLOW)

Une hirondelle ne fait pas le printemps
A swallow does not make the spring

☞ *A swallow doesn't make the summer*

HISSER (TO HOIST)

Hissez le grand perroquet !
Hoist the big parrot !

☞ *Up the top gallant sail !*

HONTE (SHAME)

J'ai rencontré Sidonie
quand j'étais avec ma vieille, la honte !
**I met Sidonie when I was
with my old, the shame !**

☞ *I met Sidonie when I was
with my mother, I was so ashamed*

HUILE (OIL)

Ça baigne dans l'huile
It is bathing in the oil

☞ *Everything is going smoothly*

HUÎTRE (OYSTER)

Je suis plein comme une huître
I am full like an oyster

☞ *I am as drunk as a lord*

Je ne supporte pas sa face d'huître
I do not stand his face of oyster

☞ *I can't stand his ugly mug*

I, J

INCENDIER (*TO BURN DOWN*)

> Je me suis fait incendier
> **I have been burnt down**
>
> ☞ *I have been caught*

INCONNU (*UNKNOWN*)

> Inconnu au bataillon
> **Unknown at the batalion**
>
> ☞ *No one's ever heard of him*

INCRUSTER (*TO INCRUST*)

> Ce soir, on va essayer de taper l'incruste
> dans une fête
> **Tonight, we are going to smack
> the incrust in a feast**
>
> ☞ *This evening we'll try and crash a party*

INDEX (*FOREFINGER*)

> Ce livre est à l'index
> **This book is at the forefinger**
>
> ☞ *This book is blacklisted*

Je me suis fait incendier
(*I have been caught*)

JAMBE (LEG)

Ça me fait une belle jambe
It makes me a nice leg

☞ *It won't get me very far*

Faire des ronds de jambes
To make rounds of legs

☞ *To bow and scrape*

JAUNE (YELLOW)

Rire jaune
To laugh yellow

☞ *To give a forced laugh*

JETER (TO THROW)

On a eu le temps de s'en mettre plein
la lampe avant de se faire jeter
**We had time to get ourselves full
the lamp before we were
thrown away**

☞ *We had enough time to stuff our faces
before we were thrown out*

JETON (CHIP)

Il lui a filé un tel jeton
qu'il ne savait plus son nom
**He thread him such a chip
that he even didn't remember
his name**

☞ *He gave him such a punch
he couldn't remember who he was*

JETON (TOKEN)

Un faux jeton
A false token

☞ *A phoney*

JEU (GAME)

Le jeu n'en vaut pas la chandelle
The game is not worth the candle

☞ *It is not worth it*

Être vieux jeu
To be old game

☞ *To be old-fashioned*

140

Rire jaune
(*To give a forced laugh*)

JEUNESSE (YOUTH)

Allez roulez jeunesse !
Go and roll youth !

☞ *Full steam ahead !*

JONC (RUSH)

Tu me pèles le jonc !
You are peeling my rush !

☞ *You get up my nose !*

JOUER (TO PLAY)

Jouer son va-tout
To play one's go all

☞ *To play one's last card*

JOUR (DAY)

Il vit au jour le jour
He lives at the day the day

☞ *He lives from hand to mouth*

JURER (TO SWEAR)

Non ? Jure ? Tu ne sors pas
avec cette erreur humaine
**No ? Swear ? You are not going out
with this human error**

☞ *No ? Honest ? You're going out
with that creep*

JUS (JUICE)

Ce café est un vrai jus de chaussettes
This coffee is a true juice of socks

☞ *It's watery coffee*

K, L

KIF (MARIJUANA)

Kif-kif bourricot
Marijuana-marijuana donkey

☞ *It is the same thing*

KIKI (NECK)

C'est parti mon kiki
It is gone my neck

☞ *Here we go*

KILLER (KILLER)

Ce type, c'est vraiment un killer
This chap, is a real killer

☞ *That guy is very dangerous*

LÀ (HERE)

Une Marie-couche-toi-là
A Mary-sleep-here

☞ *A tart*

LAC (LAKE)

Il n'y a pas le feu au lac
There is not fire at the lake

☞ *We are not in a hurry*

LÂCHER (TO DROP)

Lâche-moi la grappe, tu me gonfles
**Drop me the cluster,
you are inflating me**

☞ *Leave me alone, you're bugging me*

LAIT (MILK)

Coquilles Saint-Jacques
ou cochon de lait ?
Shells holy James or pig of milk ?

☞ *Scallops or sucking pig ?*

LANCE-PIERRE (CATAPULT)

J'ai mangé avec un lance-pierre
I ate with a catapult

☞ *I grabbed a quick bite*

Kif kif bourricot
(*It is the same thing*)

LANGUE (*TONGUE*)

Langue vivante
Living tongue

☞ *A spoken language*

Avoir une langue bien pendue
To have a well hanged tongue

☞ *A chatter box*

Je donne ma langue au chat
I give my tongue to the cat

☞ *I give up*

C'est une mauvaise langue
She is a bad tongue

☞ *She is tittle-tattle*

LAPIN (*RABBIT*)

Quel chaud lapin !
What a hot rabbit !

☞ *What a horny bugger !*

Haut les mains, peau de lapin !
High the hands, skin of rabbit !

☞ *Hands up !*

Poser un lapin
To put down a rabbit
☞ *To stand someone up*

LARD *(BACON)*

C'est du lard ou du cochon ?
Is it bacon or pig ?
☞ *You never know where you are with him*

LARGE *(WIDE)*

Ne pas en mener large
Not to lead wide
☞ *To be scared*

LARGUER *(TO RELEASE)*

Jo la Banane s'est fait larguer
par sa meuf
**Jo the Banana has been released
by his manwo**
☞ *Jo the Banana's wife has left him*

LARRON (*ROBBER*)

S'entendre comme larrons en foire
To hear each other like robbers in fair

☞ *To get on well together*

LÉGUME (*VEGETABLE*)

Une grosse légume
A big vegetable

☞ *A V.I.P.*

LESSIVER (*TO WASH*)

Le sport, ça me lessive trop
**The sport, it washes myself
too much**

☞ *Sport is too tiring for me*

LETTRE (*LETTER*)

Au pied de la lettre
At the foot of the letter

☞ *Literally*

Avoir des lettres
To have letters

☞ *A cultivated person*

LEVER (*TO LIFT*)

Lever le coude
To lift the elbow

☞ *To drink a lot*

LÉZARD (*LIZARD*)

Il n'y a pas de lézard
There is no lizard

☞ *There's no problem*

LIEU (*PLACE*)

J'ai tout lieu de croire
I have all place to believe

☞ *Everything leads me to believe*

LIÈVRE (*HARE*)

Soulever un lièvre
To lift up a hare

☞ *To stir up a hornet's nest*

LIGNE (*LINE*)

Entrer en ligne de compte
To enter in line of count

☞ *To enter into consideration*

LIMANDE (*DAB*)

Plate comme une limande
Flat like a dab

☞ *Flat-chested*

LION (*LION*)

Tu as bouffé du lion ou quoi ?
Did you eat lion or what ?

☞ *Are you full of beans ?*

LIT (*BED*)

C'est un enfant d'un autre lit
He is a child of an other bed

☞ *He is the child from a previous marriage*

154

Soulever un lièvre
(*To stir up a hornet's nest*)

LOUCHE (LADLE)

Il m'a serré la louche
He gripped my ladle

☞ *He shook my hand*

LOUP (WOLF)

Il est connu comme le loup blanc
He is known like the white wolf

☞ *He is very well known*

J'ai une faim de loup
I have a hunger of wolf

☞ *I could eat a horse*

LOURD (HEAVY)

Ne pas en savoir lourd
Not to know heavy about

☞ *Not to know much about*

LUNE (MOON)

Il est con comme la lune
He is stupid like the moon

☞ *He is a prize dickhead*

M

MÂCHER *(TO CHEW)*

Ne pas mâcher ses mots
Not to chew one's words

☞ *No to mince words*

MAILLE *(STITCH)*

Avoir maille à partir
To have stitch to leave

☞ *To have a bone to pick with*

MAIN *(HAND)*

Haut la main
High the hand

☞ *Easily*

Une petite main
A small hand

☞ *A dressmaker's apprentice*

Prends-toi en mains c'est ton destin !
**Take yourself in your hands,
it's your destiny !**

☞ *Pull yourself together ! You're in control
of your future !*

MAIS (BUT)

Il n'y a pas de mais !
There is no but !

☞ *I don't want to hear it !*

MAISON (HOUSE)

C'est gros comme une maison
It is big like a house

☞ *It is as plain as the nose on your face*

MAÎTRE (MASTER)

Pour un coup d'essai, c'est un coup
de maître
**For a blow of try, it is a blow
of master**

☞ *It is a very good first attempt*

MAL (BAD)

Avoir le mal du pays
To have the bad of the country

☞ *To be homesick*

160

Être mal en point
To be bad in point

☞ *To be poorly*

Faire mal à quelqu'un
To do bad to somebody

☞ *To hurt someone*

Je me suis donné un mal de chien
I gave myself a bad of dog

☞ *I bent over backwards*

Dis pas ça, tu te fais du mal
**Don't say that, you are making
yourself bad**

☞ *Don't be so pessimistic*

MALAISE (*DISCOMFORT*)

J'te raconte pas le malaise quand je l'ai vu
**I don't tell you the discomfort
when I saw him**

☞ *I felt very uncomfortable when I saw him*

MALHEUR (BAD LUCK)

Faire un malheur
To do a bad luck

☞ *To be very successful*

MALLE (TRUNK)

On se fait la malle, c'est trop galère ici
**We make the trunk,
it is too slave ship here**

☞ *Let's get out of here, it's such a bore*

MANCHE (SLEEVE)

La première manche
The first sleeve

☞ *The first set*

MANDAT (MONEY-ORDER)

Un mandat d'amener
A money-order to bring

☞ *Writ of arrest*

Un avocat marron
(*A shady lawyer*)

MANGER (FAMILIER : BOUFFER) (TO EAT)

Culottes bouffantes
Eating pants

☞ *Baggy pants*

MARCHE (STEP)

Mettre en marche
To put in step

☞ *To start up*

MARCHER (TO WALK)

Faire marcher à la baguette
To make walk at the stick

☞ *To rule someone with a rod of iron*

MARI (HUSBAND)

Ciel mon mari !
Sky my husband !

☞ *My god ! My husband !*

MARIAGE (MARRIAGE)

C'est le mariage de la carpe et du lapin
**It is the marriage of the carp
and the rabbit**

☞ *They are unlikely bed fellows*

MARRON (BROWN)

Un avocat marron
A brown avocado

☞ *A shady lawyer*

MARTEAU (HAMMER)

Être marteau
To be hammer

☞ *To be crazy*

MASSE (MASS)

J'ai rarement vu quelqu'un être autant
à la masse
**I have rarely seen somebody to be
as much at the mass**

☞ *I've rarely seen someone that crazy*

MÉCANIQUE (*MECHANICAL*)

Tiens ! Voilà le rouleur de mécaniques
qui ramène sa fraise
**Hold ! here is the roller
of mechanicals who brings back
his strawberry**

☞ *Well ! here comes that show-off*

MÈCHE (*WICK*)

Être de mèche
To be of wick

☞ *To be in cahoots*

MEILLEUR (*BEST*)

J'en passe, et des meilleures !
I am passing some, and of the best !

☞ *And that's not all !*

MÊME (*SAME*)

C'est du pareil au même
It is the same to the same

☞ *To be as broad as it is long*

166

MÉNAGE (CLEANING)

Se mettre en ménage
To put oneself in cleaning

☞ *To set up house together*

Ménage à trois
Cleaning at three

☞ *Matrimonial triangle*

MÉNAGER (TO HANDLE)

Il ménage la chèvre et le chou
**He handles the goat
and the cabbage**

☞ *He sits on the fence*

MER (SEA)

Ce n'est pas la mer à boire
It is not the sea to drink

☞ *It is not that difficult*

MERCI (THANK YOU)

Il a sa femme à sa merci
He has his wife at his thank you

☞ *His wife is at his mercy*

MERDE (*SHIT*)

> Il est dans la merde jusqu'au cou
> **He is in the shit up to the neck**
>
>> ☞ *He is up shit creek without a paddle*

MÈRE (*MOTHER*)

> Rentre chez ta mère !
> **Go back to your mother !**
>
>> ☞ *Piss off !*

MERLAN (*WHITING*)

> Il a des yeux de merlan frit
> **He has eyes of fried whiting**
>
>> ☞ *He is gobsmacked*

MÉTRO (*UNDERGROUND*)

> Métro, boulot, dodo
> **Underground, grind, beddy-byes**
>
>> ☞ *It's the same old routine day in, day out*

METTRE *(TO PUT)*

Sauver la mise
To save the put

☞ *To get back one's outlay*

MEUBLER *(TO FURNISH)*

Il sait meubler la conversation
**He knows how to furnish
the conversation**

☞ *He knows how to fill the blanks
of a conversation*

MICHE *(LOAF)*

On se caille les miches
We curdle the loaves

☞ *We are freezing the arse off*

MIDI *(NOON)*

Ne cherche pas midi à quatorze heures
Don't look for noon at two o'clock

☞ *Don't complicate the issue*

MINUTE (MINUTE)

Utilisez-vous une cocotte-minute ?
Do you use a chicken-minute ?

☞ *Do you use a pressure cooker ?*

MODE (FASHION)

J'adore le bœuf mode
I love the beef fashion

☞ *I love stewed beef with carrots*

MOINE (MONK)

L'habit ne fait pas le moine
Clothe doesn't make the monk

☞ *Do not judge by appearances*

MONDE (WORLD)

Il y a du monde au balcon
There is some world at the balcony

☞ *Big busted*

MONSIEUR (GENTLEMAN)

Un croque-monsieur
A bite-gentleman

☞ *A toasted ham and cheese sandwich*

MONTER (TO GO UP)

Monter en épingle
To go up in pin

☞ *To make a mountain out of a molehill*

MORDRE (TO BITE)

Mords-y l'œil, t'auras la queue !
Bite him the eye, you will get the tail !

☞ *Kill him !*

MORT (DEATH)

À l'article de la mort
At the article of the death

☞ *At the point of death*

MORUE (COD)

À sa place, je n'oserais pas sortir avec
une morue pareille
**In his place, I would not dare to go out
with such a cod**

☞ *If I were he, I wouldn't dare to go out
with that cow*

MOT (WORD)

Toucher un mot
To touch a word

☞ *To mention*

Ne pas dire un traître mot
Not to say a traitor word

☞ *Not to say a single word*

MOUCHE (FLY)

Prendre la mouche
To take the fly

☞ *To get huffy*

172

Faire mouche
To do fly

☞ *To hit the bull's eye*

Être une fine mouche
To be a fine fly

☞ *Sly minx*

Il n'arrête pas d'enculer les mouches
He keeps on sodomising the flies

☞ *He keeps spliting hairs*

Les tomber comme des mouches
To fall them like flies

☞ *To get all the girls*

MOUCHER (*TO BLOW ONE'S NOSE*)

Il ne se mouche pas du pied
**He doesn't blow his nose
with his foot**

☞ *He thinks highly of himself*

173

MOUCHOIR (HANDKERCHIEF)

Les coureurs sont arrivés
dans un mouchoir
The racers arrived in a handkerchief

☞ *The racers had a close finish*

MOUETTE (GULL)

Vos gueules les mouettes !
Shut up the gulls !

☞ *Keep quite !*

MOURIR (TO DIE)

Mourir à petit feu
To die at little fire

☞ *To fade away*

Plus nul, tu meurs
More zero, you die

☞ *It can't be worse than that*

Va mourir !
Go and die !

☞ *Leave ! You're getting on my nerves*

174

Mur (WALL)

Raser les murs
To shave the walls

☞ *To be hangdog*

Mûr (RIPE)

En dire des vertes et des pas mûres
To tell green and not ripe

☞ *To tell everything*

Musique (MUSIC)

Musique de chambre ou messe en si ?
Music of bedroom or mass in if ?

☞ *Chamber music or B mass ?*

N

NAVET (*TURNIP*)

J'ai vu un film qui était un vrai navet
I saw a film which was a real turnip

☞ *I saw a film which was a piece of rubbish*

NERF (*NERVE*)

J'ai les nerfs à fleur de peau
I have nerves at flower of skin

☞ *I am edgy*

NEVEU (*NEPHEW*)

Je veux, mon neveu !
I want, my nephew !

☞ *You bet !*

NEZ (*NOSE*)

Faire un pied de nez
To make a foot of nose

☞ *To thumb your nose*

Il a gagné les doigts dans le nez
He won the fingers in the nose

☞ *He won with his eyes closed*

Mener quelqu'un par le bout du nez
To lead someone by the end of the nose

☞ *To twist someone around one's little finger*

NICKEL (*NICKEL*)

C'est nickel chrome !
It's nickel chromium !

☞ *It's brilliant !*

NIVEAU (*LEVEL*)

Au niveau du vécu, ça m'interpelle quelque part
At the level of the lived, it is something which call me upon somewhere

☞ *That's something which I find interesting*

Il a gagné les doigts dans le nez
(*He won with his eyes closed*)

NŒUD (KNOT)

À la mords-moi le nœud
At the bite me the knot

☞ *Dodgy*

Un sac de nœuds
A bag of knots

☞ *A problem*

C'est une vraie tête de nœud !
He is a real head of knot !

☞ *He is dickhead !*

NOIR (BLACK)

Broyer du noir
To crush black

☞ *To be depressed*

Un œil au beurre noir
An eye at the black butter

☞ *A black eye*

NOM (NAME)

Un nom à coucher dehors
A name to sleep outside

☞ *An impossible name*

182

NOUILLE (*NOODLE*)

Pour les examens, il a le cul bordé
de nouilles
**For the exams, he has the ass
bordered by noodles**

☞ *He's always lucky at exams*

NU (*NAKED*)

Je suis tombé des nues
I fell from the naked

☞ *I was completely taken aback*

Porter aux nues
To bring to the naked

☞ *To praise to the skies*

NUMÉRO (*NUMBER*)

Être un drôle de numéro
To be a funny number

☞ *To be a strange character*

O

OBÉIR (*TO OBEY*)

J'aime être obéi au doigt et à l'œil
I love to be obeyed at the finger and the eye

☞ *I love it when people are at my beck and call*

ODEUR (*SMELL*)

En odeur de sainteté
In smell of holiness

☞ *In somebody's good graces*

ŒIL (*EYE*)

Avoir le coup d'œil
To have the blow of eye

☞ *To have a good eye*

Œil de bœuf
Eye of beef

☞ *A round dormer window*

Coûter les yeux de la tête
To cost the eyes of the head

☞ *To be very expensive*

187

Mon œil !
My eye !

☞ *My foot !*

Je m'en bats l'œil !
I am beating my eye !

☞ *I don't give a damn !*

Attention les yeux !
Be careful the eyes !

☞ *Look out*

Bon pied, bon œil
Good foot, good eye

☞ *To be in good health*

Faire de l'œil
To make eye

☞ *To give someone the eye*

ŒUF (EGG)

Va te faire cuire un œuf !
Go and make you cook an egg !

☞ *Go fly a kite !*

ŒUVRE (WORK)

Un chef-d'œuvre
A chief of work

☞ A masterpiece

OIE (GOOSE)

Il habite à Trifouillis-les-Oies
He lives at Trifouillis-the-Geese

☞ He lives at nowhere city

Une oie blanche
A white goose

☞ A silly girl

OIGNONS (ONIONS)

Ce n'est pas tes oignons
It is not your onions

☞ It's none of your business

OR (GOLD)

J'en connais qui se font des couilles en or
**I know some ones who are making
themselves golden testicles**

☞ I know some people who make piles
of money

OREILLE (EAR)

Avoir la puce à l'oreille
To have the flea at the ear

☞ *To suspect*

OS (BONE)

Tomber sur un os
To fall down on a bone

☞ *To hit a problem*

Cette fois-ci, tu l'as dans l'os
That time, you get it in the bone

☞ *You're screwed this time*

OUI (YES)

Un béni oui-oui
A blessed yes-yes

☞ *A yes-man*

OURS (BEAR)

C'est un ours mal léché
He is a bad licked bear

☞ *He is an uncouth fellow*

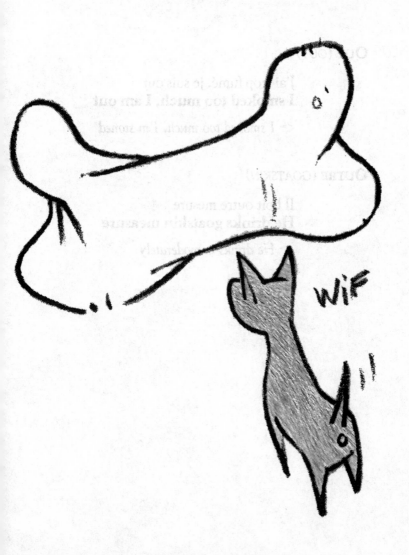

Tomber sur un os
(*To hit a problem*)

OUT (OUT)

J'ai trop fumé, je suis out
I smoked too much, I am out

☞ *I smoked too much, I'm stoned*

OUTRE (GOATSKIN)

Il boit outre mesure
He drinks goatskin measure

☞ *He drinks immoderately*

P

Pain (BREAD)

Ça ne mange pas de pain
It doesn't eat bread

☞ *It is not important*

J'ai mangé mon pain blanc
I have eaten my white bread

☞ *The worse is still ahead*

Pain perdu ou pain complet ?
Lost bread or complete bread ?

☞ *Wholemeal bread or french toast ?*

Panier (BASKET)

Il lui a mis la main au panier
He put his hand at her basket

☞ *He pinched her bum*

Papier (PAPER)

Être dans les petits papiers de quelqu'un
**To be in the little papers
of somebody**

☞ *To be in somebody's good books*

195

PAPILLON (*BUTTERFLY*)

Minute papillon !
Minute butterfly !

☞ *Hold it now !*

PÂQUERETTE (*DAISY*)

Il est au ras des pâquerettes
He is short to the daisies

☞ *He is very basic*

PAQUET (*PACKAGE*)

Mettre le paquet
To put the package

☞ *To pull out all the stops*

PARFUM (*PERFUME*)

Être au parfum
To be at the perfume

☞ *To be aware of*

196

PARLER *(TO SPEAK)*

Parler à bâtons rompus
To speak at broken sticks

☞ *To speak a lot*

Tu parles Charles !
You speak Charles !

☞ *You don't say !*

J'en parlerai à mon cheval
I will speak to my horse

☞ *You bet !*

Parle à mon cul ma tête est malade !
Talk to my ass my head is sick !

☞ *Fuck off and leave me alone !*

PASSER *(TO PASS)*

Passer sur le billard
To pass on the billard

☞ *To have an operation*

Passer à la casserole
To pass in the pan

☞ *To be killed or to get laid*

197

PÂTÉ (*PIE*)

Quand je ne dors pas assez,
je suis dans le pâté toute la journée
When I do not sleep enough,
I am in the pie all the day

☞ *When I can't get enough sleep,*
I'm groggy all day

PATIN (*SKATE*)

J'aimerais bien lui rouler un patin
I would like to roll her a skate

☞ *I'd like to kiss her (him)*

PÊCHE (*PEACH*)

Je n'ai pas la pêche
I do not have the peach

☞ *I am a bit down*

On s'est fendu la pêche
We have split the peach

☞ *We were in stitches*

En ce moment, j'ai la méga pêche
I have the super peach
at this moment

☞ *I'm in top form at the moment*

PÉDALER (*TO PEDAL*)

> Pédaler dans la choucroute
> **To pedal in the sauerkraut**
>
> ☞ *To be mixed up*

PEIGNE (*COMB*)

> Quel peigne cul ce type !
> **What a comb ass this guy !**
>
> ☞ *What a redneck !*

PEINTURE (*PAINTING*)

> Ne pas pouvoir voir quelqu'un
> en peinture
> **Not be able to see somebody
> in painting**
>
> ☞ *To hate somebody*

PELLE (*SHOVEL*)

> Je lui ai roulé une pelle
> **I rolled her a shovel**
>
> ☞ *I swapped spits*

Ils sont ronds comme des queues
de pelle
They are round like tails of shovel

☞ *They are drunk as skunks*

PELLICULE *(FILM)*

Avoir des pellicules
To have films

☞ *To have dandruff*

(SE) PENCHER *(TO LEAN)*

Avoir un penchant pour quelqu'un
To have a leaning for someone

☞ *To fancy someone*

PENDULE *(CLOCK)*

Tu vas pas nous chier une pendule...
**You are not going to shit us
a clock...**

☞ *You are not going to make a fuss
about it...*

PENSER (TO THINK)

> Un pense-bête
> **A think-silly**
>
> ☞ *A reminder*

PERDRE (TO LOSE)

> Perdre la boule
> **To lose the bowl**
>
> ☞ *To go crazy*

PET (FART)

> Ça ne vaut pas un pet de lapin
> **It isn't worth a fart of rabbit**
>
> ☞ *It's worthless*
>
> Face de pet !
> **Face of fart !**
>
> ☞ *You dolt !*

PÉTARD (CRACKER)

> Il est en pétard
> **He is in cracker**
>
> ☞ *He is fuming*

201

PÉTARD (CRACK)

Après avoir fumé un pétard
j'ai la tête comme une citrouille
After having smoked a crack
I have the head like a pumpkin

☞ *After having smoked a joint, I'm out of it*

PETIT (LITTLE)

Au petit bonheur, la chance
At the little luck, the chance

☞ *At random*

PHOQUE (SEAL)

Il est pédé comme un phoque
He is queer like a seal

☞ *He is a ragging queer*

PHOTO (PICTURE)

Tu veux ma photo ?
Do you want my picture ?

☞ *What are you looking at ?*

PIANO (*PIANO*)

Puis-je jouer du piano à queue ?
May I play piano with tail ?

☞ *May I play the grand piano ?*

PIÈCE (*COIN*)

Pièce rapportée
Brought-back coin

☞ *Relation by marriage*

PIED (*FOOT*)

À cloche-pied
At bell-foot

☞ *To hop*

De pied en cap
From foot to cape

☞ *Elegant*

Un casse-pieds
A break-feet

☞ *A bore*

203

Prendre son pied
To take one's foot

☞ *To have it away*

Elle vit sur un grand pied
She lives on a big foot

☞ *She lives on a grand scale*

C'est le pied
It is the foot

☞ *It's great*

Au pied de la lettre
At the foot of the letter

☞ *Literally*

Ne pas savoir sur quel pied danser
No to know on which foot to dance

☞ *Not to know how to behave*

PILE (*BATTERY*)

Tomber pile
To fall battery

☞ *To happen at the right moment*

204

PINCETTES (PAIR OF TONGS)

Il n'est pas à prendre avec des pincettes
He is not to be taken with a pair of tongs

☞ *He is like a bear with a sore head*

PIPE (PIPE)

Nom d'une pipe !
Name of a pipe !

☞ *My god !*

Il a cassé sa pipe
He broke his pipe

☞ *He kicked the bucket*

PIPEAU (REED PIPE)

C'est du pipeau
It's reed pipe

☞ *That's a lot of rubbish*

PLAISANTERIE (JOKE)

Une plaisanterie de corps de garde
A joke of body of guard

☞ *An off-colour joke*

205

PLAN (MAP)

Cette fille est un mauvais plan,
elle est baguée
This girl is a bad map, she is ringed

☞ *She's not worth the trouble,*
the girl is engaged

Samedi on a zoné toute la soirée,
c'était vraiment un plan loose
Saturday we have zoned
all the night, it was truly a map loose

☞ *We wasted our time wandering around*
on Saturday night

PLANCHE (BOARD)

Plancher
To board

☞ *To be called up to the blackboard*

Une planche pourrie
A rotten board

☞ *A dubious character*

Il y a encore du pain sur la planche
There is still bread on the board

☞ *There is still a lot to do*

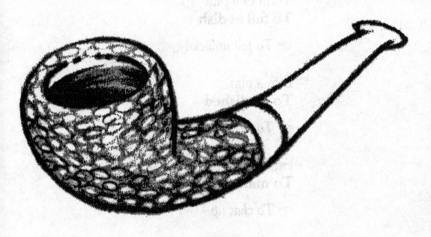

Ceci est une pipe. Elle s'appelle Zézette

Nom d'une pipe
(My god !)

PLANTER (*TO PLANT*)

Se planter
To plant oneself

☞ *To fail*

PLAT (*DISH*)

Tomber à plat
To fall at dish

☞ *To fall unluckily*

Être à plat
To be dished

☞ *To be washed out*

Faire du plat à quelqu'un
To make dish to somebody

☞ *To chat up*

Je crois que j'ai mis les pieds dans le plat
I think I put the feet in the dish

☞ *I think I spilled the beans*

Il m'en a fait tout un plat
He made me all a dish of it

☞ *He made a song and dance about it*

PLAT (FLAT)

Battre à plate couture
To beat at flat seam

☞ *To beat someone hollow*

PLEIN (FULL)

En mettre plein la vue
To put full of sight

☞ *To dazzle someone*

Ils sont pleins comme des huîtres
They are full like oysters

☞ *They are bombed*

PLI (FOLD)

Ça ne fait pas un pli
It doesn't make a fold

☞ *No doubt about it*

PLIER (TO FOLD)

Plier bagage
To fold luggage

☞ *To leave*

Il était tellement givré que j'étais plié
He was so much frosty
that I was fold

☞ *He was so crazy that I was splitting*
my sides with laughter

PLUIE (RAIN)

Il n'est pas né de la dernière pluie
He is not born from the last rain

☞ *He wasn't born yesterday*

POCHE (POCKET)

Il n'a pas les yeux dans sa poche
He hasn't got his eyes in his pocket

☞ *He is very clued in*

POÊLE (STOVE)

Comment vas-tu yau d'poêle ?
How are you pipe of stove ?

☞ *What's up doc ?*

210

POIL (HAIR)

Être à poil
To be at hair

☞ *To be naked*

Reprendre du poil de la bête
**To take back the hair
from the beast**

☞ *To be one's own self again*

On s'est vachement poilé
We cowly haired ourselves

☞ *We laughed a lot*

POINTER (TO POINT)

Quand elle s'est pointée,
j'ai trop halluciné
**When she pointed herself,
I was too much hallucinated**

☞ *When she arrived I was completely
fascinated*

POIRE (PEAR)

C'est bien fait pour sa poire
It is well made for his pear

☞ *It is one in eye for him*

Il a pris une pêche en pleine poire
He took a peach in full pear

☞ *He got clocked right in the dial*

Entre la poire et le fromage
Between the pear and the cheese

☞ *At the end of a meal*

Ne me prends pas pour une poire, William
Don't take me for a pear, William

☞ *Don't take me for a sucker, William*

POIREAU (LEEK)

Faire le poireau
To make the leek

☞ *To wait for someone*

POIS (PEA)

Pois cassés ou pommes pont-neuf ?
Broken peas or apples new bridge ?

☞ *Split peas or pommes pont-neuf ?*

POISSON (FISH)

Elle m'a engueulé comme
du poisson pourri
**She gave out to me like
to a rotten fish**

☞ *She called me all the names under the sun*

POMME (APPLE)

Il est haut comme trois pommes
He is high like three apples

☞ *He is knee-high to a grasshopper*

Bien fait pour ta pomme !
Well made for your apple !

☞ *It serves you right !*

Je suis tombé dans les pommes
I fell in the apples

☞ *I fainted*

POMPE (PUMP)

Aller à toute pompe
To go at all pump

☞ To go very fast

Il est à côté de ses pompes
He is at the side of his pumps

☞ He is out of his mind

POMPER (TO PUMP)

Tu commences à me pomper l'air
You start to pump me the air

☞ You're beginning to annoy me

J'ai rarement vu une nana
aussi pompante
**I have rarely seen a girl
as much pumping**

☞ I've rarely seen a girl that encroaching

PONT (BRIDGE)

Tu fais le pont ?
You make the bridge ?

☞ Are you making a long week end of it ?

PORT (*HARBOUR*)

> Un port de reine
> **A harbour of queen**
>
> ☞ *A queenly bearing*

PORTRAIT (*PICTURE*)

> Un portrait tout craché
> **A picture all spat**
>
> ☞ *The spitting image*

POSER (*TO PUT DOWN*)

> Poser un lapin
> **To put down a rabbit**
>
> ☞ *To stand someone up*

POSITIVER (*TO POSITIVE*)

> Quand la vie c'est cool, je positive
> **When life is cool, I positive**
>
> ☞ *When life is going well, I'm in good form*

POSTE (MAIL)

Rejoindre son poste
To go back to one's mail

☞ *To rejoin one's regiment*

POT (POT)

Un pot-au-feu
A pot at the fire

☞ *Hot pot*

Pot de vin
Pot of wine

☞ *A backhander*

Avoir du pot
To have pot

☞ *To be lucky*

Qui va payer les pots cassés ?
**Who is going to pay
for the broken pots ?**

☞ *Who is going to face the music ?*

POTAGE (*SOUP*)

Il y a une couille dans le potage.
Bonjour les dégâts !
There is a testicle in the soup.
Good morning the damages !

☞ *There's trouble here.*
Things don't look good !

POUCE (*THUMB*)

Pouce !
Thumb !

☞ *Pax !*

Dîner sur le pouce
To dine on the thumb

☞ *To have a quick bite to eat*

POULE (*CHICKEN*)

Pied-de-poule
Foot of chicken

☞ *Dog tooth check*

Une poule mouillée
A wet chicken

☞ *A coward*

217

Poule de luxe
Luxurious chicken

☞ *A high class call girl*

Chair de poule
Flesh of chicken

☞ *Goose flesh*

Alors ma poule ça gaze ?
Then my hen it gases ?

☞ *How are you doing honey ?*

POULET (CHICKEN)

Et mon cul, c'est du poulet !
And my ass, it is chicken !

☞ *What a load of crap !*

POURRIR (TO ROT)

Manu, il s'est fait pourrir sur 400 mètres
avec sa poubelle
**Manu has been rotten on 400 meters
with his garbage**

☞ *Manu was overtaken in less than 400 m
in his old jalopy*

218

POUSSER (*TO PUSH*)

> À la va-comme-je-te-pousse
> **At the go like I push you**
>
> ☞ *Any which way*

PRALINE (*SUGAR ALMOND*)

> Quel culcul la praline !
> **What an ass ass the sugar almond**
>
> ☞ *What a sissy !*

PRENDRE (*TO TAKE*)

> Tu me prends le chou
> **You take me the cabbage**
>
> ☞ *You're a pain in the ass*

> Prise de tête
> **Taken of head**
>
> ☞ *That's a real pain*

PRESSER (*TO PRESS*)

> Il me presse le citron
> **He is pressing my lemon**
>
> ☞ *He is beating my brain*

PRISE (*PLUG*)

Une prise de bec
A plug of beak

☞ *An argument*

PROCHAIN (*NEXT*)

Aimer son prochain
To love one's next

☞ *To love one's neighbour*

PROPRE (*CLEAN*)

C'est du propre !
It is clean !

☞ *Well done ! (ironical)*

Un propre à rien
A clean to nothing

☞ *A no-good*

Il l'a fait de son propre chef
He made it of his clean chief

☞ *He did it of his own accord*

Il n'a aucun amour propre
He doesn't have any clean love

☞ *He doesn't have any self respect*

PROTESTER *(TO PROTEST)*

J'ai protesté comme un beau diable
I protested like a beautiful devil

☞ *I protested for all I was worth*

PRUNE *(PLUM)*

Je te paie des prunes !
I pay you plums !

☞ *I'll eat my hat !*

Il travaille pour des prunes
He works for plums

☞ *He works for peanuts*

PUR *(PURE)*

Je suis allé à un pur concert
I went to a pure concert

☞ *I went to a brilliant concert*

Q, R

QUART (*QUARTER*)

> Au quart de tour
> **At the quarter of turn**
>
> ☞ *Immediately*

QUATORZE (*FOURTEEN*)

> C'est parti comme en quatorze
> **It is gone like in fourteen**
>
> ☞ *It's started well*

QUATRE (*FOUR*)

> Se mettre en quatre
> **To put oneself in four**
>
> ☞ *To bend over backwards*

QUELQU'UN (*SOMEBODY*)

> Avoir quelqu'un à la bonne
> **To have somebody at the good**
>
> ☞ *To be fond of somebody*

QUEUE (TAIL)

Il tire le diable par la queue
He pulls out the devil by the tail

☞ *He lives from hand to mouth*

RACCOURCIR (TO SHORTEN)

Il m'est tombé dessus à bras raccourcis
He felt on me at shorten arms

☞ *He pitched into me*

RADAR (RADAR)

Avant 11 heures du mat, je marche
au radar
**Before eleven in the morn, I walk
with the radar**

☞ *Before eleven a.m., I'm not awake*

RADIS (RADISH)

J'ai plus un radis
I have no more radish

☞ *I do not have a bean left*

RAIDE (TIGHT)

Je me suis enfilé tellement de tequila
rapido que j'suis raide dead
**I thread myself so much tequila
rapido that I am tight dead**

☞ *I drank so much Tequila
I'm completely gone*

RAISIN (GRAPE)

Mi-figue, mi-raisin
Half-fig, half-grape

☞ *Neither fish nor fowl*

RAMASSER (TO PICK UP)

Être à ramasser à la petite cuiller
To be to pick up at a little spoon

☞ *To be exhausted*

RAMER (TO ROW)

On a ramé comme des bêtes
sur ce projet
**We have rowed like beasts
on this project**

☞ *We worked hard on this project*

RAPPORT (*REPORT*)

Avoir des rapports sexuels
To have sexual reports

☞ *To have sexual relations*

RAT (*RAT*)

Être fait comme un rat
To be made like a rat

☞ *To be done for*

RAYER (*TO SCRATCH*)

Un complet rayé
A scratched complete

☞ *A pin striped suit*

Rayé des cadres
Scratched from the frames

☞ *Struck off the list*

RAYON (*X RAY*)

En connaître un rayon
To know one X ray

☞ *To know a lot*

228

RECETTE *(RECIPE)*

> Faire recette
> **To make recipe**
>
> ☞ *To take money (for a theater)*

REGARD *(LOOK)*

> Couler un regard
> **To flow a look**
>
> ☞ *To cast a glance*

REGARDER *(TO LOOK)*

> Il n'est pas regardant
> **He is not looking**
>
> ☞ *He is not fussy*

RÉGIME *(DIET)*

> Un régime de bananes
> **A bananas diet**
>
> ☞ *A bunch of bananas*

RÉGLÉ (ORDERED)

C'est réglé comme du papier musique
It is ordered like music paper

☞ *It is ordered like clockwork*

REIN (KIDNEY)

Un tour de reins
A turn of kidneys

☞ *A sudden back pain*

REINE (QUEEN)

Je voudrais une bouchée à la reine
I would like a fill up to the queen

☞ *I would like a chicken vol-au-vent*

RENVOYER (TO SEND BACK)

Faire un renvoi
To make a sent back

☞ *To belch*

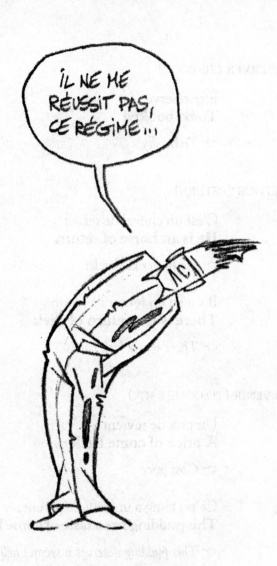

Un régime de bananes
(*A bunch of bananas*)

RÉSERVER (*TO BOOK*)

Être réservé
To be booked

☞ *To be shy*

RETOUR (*RETURN*)

C'est un cheval de retour
He is an horse of return

☞ *He is an old chiseler*

Il y a eu un retour de bâton
There was a return of stick

☞ *There was a kick back*

REVENIR (*TO COME BACK*)

Un prix de revient
A price of come back

☞ *Cost price*

Ce pudding a un goût de revenez-y
This pudding has a taste of come back

☞ *This pudding deserves a second helping*

RHUME (*COLD*)

Un rhume carabiné
A rifled cold

☞ *A bad cold*

RIDEAU (*CURTAIN*)

Grimper aux rideaux
To climb to the curtains

☞ *To thoroughly enjoy something*

RINCER (*TO RINSE*)

Se rincer la dalle
To rinse one's paving stone

☞ *To wet one's whistle*

RIRE (*TO LAUGH*)

C'est un pince sans rire
He is a pinch without laugh

☞ *He is a very deadpan*

233

ROCHE (ROCK)

Il y a anguille sous roche
There is eel under the rock

☞ *I smell a rat*

ROND (ROUND)

Rond comme une queue de pelle
Round like a tail of shovel

☞ *Very drunk*

J'ai plus un rond, style Armée du Salut
I have no more round, style Army of Hello

☞ *I have no more money*

RONGER (TO GNAW)

Ronger son frein
To gnaw one's brake

☞ *To champ at the bit*

ROUE (WHEEL)

Sur les chapeaux de roue
On the hats of wheels

☞ *Very fast*

ROUGE *(RED)*

Du gros rouge
Some big red

☞ *Cheap red wine*

ROULER *(TO ROLL)*

On s'en roule un
Let's roll one

☞ *Let's smoke a joint*

ROUTE *(ROAD)*

Un dernier pour la route
A last one for the road

☞ *A last drink*

RUE *(STREET)*

Ça ne court pas les rues
It doesn't run the streets

☞ *To be rare*

S

SABLE (*SAND*)

> Sabler le champagne
> **To sand the champagne**
>
> ☞ *To celebrate*

SABOT (*CLOG*)

> Je le vois venir avec ses gros sabots
> **I see him coming with his big clogs**
>
> ☞ *I can see just what he is*

SAC (*BAG*)

> Mettre à sac
> **To put to bag**
>
> ☞ *To rifle*

> On l'a pris la main dans le sac
> **We took him the hand in the bag**
>
> ☞ *He was caught red handed*

SALADE (*SALAD*)

> Il nous a raconté des salades
> **He told us salads**
>
> ☞ *He told us fibs*

SALUT (HELLO)

Une planche de salut
A board of hello

☞ A life line

Je vais finir à l'Armée du Salut
**I am going to finish at the Army
of Hello**

☞ I will end up at the Salvation Army

SANTÉ (HEALTH)

À votre santé
At your health

☞ Sheers

SAPER (TO SAP)

Ce mec est super bien sapé
This guy is super well sapped

☞ That guy is really well dressed

SAVON (SOAP)

Passer un savon
To pass a soap

☞ To shout at

SCIER (*TO SAW*)

Ça m'a scié !
It sawed me !

☞ *You could have knocked me down with a feather !*

SEC (*DRY*)

Quand je l'ai vu, je suis parti aussi sec
When I saw him, I left also dry

☞ *When I saw him, I immediately left*

Je sèche souvent les cours
I often dry the courses

☞ *I often skip classes*

SECOND (*SECOND*)

C'est un second couteau
He is a second knife

☞ *He is a minor figure*

SECOUER (*TO SHAKE*)

Rien à secouer
Nothing to shake

☞ *It is not my problem*

SENS (*WAY*)

Avoir du bon sens
To have good way

☞ *To be sensible*

SERRER (*TO SQUEEZE*)

Je me suis fait encore serrer par les bleus
**I have been again squeezed
by the blues**

☞ *I got stopped by the police again*

SIÈGE (*SEAT*)

Faire le siège
To make the seat

☞ *To lay siege to*

État de siège
State of seat

☞ *Siege*

Siège social
Social seat

☞ *Registered office*

SIFFLET (WHISTLE)

Il m'a coupé le sifflet
He cut me the whistle

☞ *He interrupted me*

SITUATION (JOB)

Résumer la situation
To resume the job

☞ *To sum up*

SŒUR (SISTER)

Et ta sœur ?
And about your sister ?

☞ *Mind your own business*

SOIF (THIRST)

Elle a gardé une poire pour la soif
She kept a pear for the thirst

☞ *She saved for a rainy day*

243

SON (*SOUND*)

> La fête bat son plein
> **The feast beats full sound**
>
> ☞ *The party is in full swing*

SONNER (*TO RING*)

> Être sonné
> **To be rung**
>
> ☞ *To be knocked out*

> On t'a pas sonné !
> **We didn't ring you !**
>
> ☞ *Nobody asked you !*

SORTIE (*WAY OUT*)

> Faire une sortie à quelqu'un
> **To make a way out to somebody**
>
> ☞ *To bawl somebody out*

SOUCI (*WORRY*)

> C'est le cadet de mes soucis
> **It is the junior of my worries**
>
> ☞ *It is the last of my problems*

Soulier (SHOE)

Être dans ses petits souliers
To be in one's little shoes

☞ *To feel awkward*

Soupe (SOUP)

J'en ai soupé de ma belle-sœur
I souped of my beautiful sister

☞ *I am fed up with my sister-in-law*

Il est arrivé comme un cheveu sur la soupe
He arrived like a hair on the soup

☞ *He turned up at the most inappropriate
moment*

Arrête de cracher dans la soupe
Stop spitting in the soup

☞ *Don't bite the hand that feeds you*

Il est très soupe-au-lait
He is very soup of milk

☞ *He flares up easily*

Un gros plein de soupe
A big full of soup

☞ *A big fat slob*

SOUPIRER (*TO SIGH*)

> Soupirer à fendre l'âme
> **To sigh to split the soul**
>
> ☞ *To sigh deeply*

SOURIS (*MOUSE*)

> Une chauve-souris
> **A bald mouse**
>
> ☞ *A bat*

STONE (*STONE*)

> Un seul pétard de pakistanaise
> et tu es complètement stone
> **Only one crack of pakistanese
> and you are completely stoned**
>
> ☞ *One Pakistani joint and you're
> completely out of it*

STYLE (*STYLE*)

> Style ! T'as acheté une nouvelle caisse
> **Style ! You did buy a new case**
>
> ☞ *Hey ! You bought yourself a new car !*

Un petit suisse
(*A soft cream cheese*)

SUCER (TO SUCK)

Il ne suce pas que des glaçons
He is not only sucking ice cubes

☞ He is often plastererd

SUCRE (SUGAR)

Je me suis fait sucrer mon permis
I got my license sugared

☞ I got my driving license pulled in

Il m'a cassé du sucre sur le dos
He broke sugar on my back

☞ He slandered me behind my back

Il sucre les fraises
He sugars the strawberries

☞ He is old and doddery

SUISSE (SWISS)

Un petit-suisse
A little Swiss

☞ A soft cream cheese

T

TABAC (TOBACCO)

C'est du même tabac
It is of the same tobacco

☞ *It is the same*

Il a fait un tabac
He made a tobacco

☞ *It was a roaring success*

TABLEAU (PAINTING)

Brosser un tableau
To brush a painting

☞ *To describe*

Jouer sur les deux tableaux
To play on the two paintings

☞ *To lay odds both ways*

TÂCHE (SPOT)

Se tuer à la tâche
To kill oneself at the spot

☞ *To kill oneself working*

TACHE (SPOT)

> T'es qu'une tache !
> **You are just a spot !**
>
> ☞ *You're a waste of time !*

TAILLER (TO CUT)

> On ferait mieux de tailler la route
> avant l'arrivée des keufs
> **We'd better cut the road
> before the cops arrive**
>
> ☞ *We'd better get out of here
> before the cops arrive*

TAMBOUR (DRUM)

> Il est arrivé sans tambour ni trompette
> **He came without drum
> and trumpet**
>
> ☞ *He came without any fuss*

TAPER (TO HIT)

> Se taper la cloche
> **To hit one's bell**
>
> ☞ *To eat well*

TAPER (*TO SMACK*)

> Dans le métro, on se fait toujours
> taper du blé
> **In the tube, we are always being
> smacked of corn**
>
> ☞ *You're always being asked for money
> in the metro*

TAPISSERIE (*TAPESTRY*)

> Faire tapisserie
> **To make tapestry**
>
> ☞ *To be a wallflower*

TARTE (*PIE*)

> Ce n'est pas de la tarte !
> **It is not pie !**
>
> ☞ *It is not easy !*

TARTINE (*TOAST*)

> Écrire des tartines
> **To write toasts**
>
> ☞ *To write a lot*

TAXER (*TO TAX*)

> Je lui ai taxé sa voiture
> **I taxed his car**
>
> ☞ *I borrowed his car*

TÉLÉPHONE (*TELEPHONE*)

> On se téléphone et on se fait une bouffe
> **We telephone ourselves**
> **and we make a puff**
>
> ☞ *We'll telephone each other and arrange*
> *to have a meal together*

TEMPS (*TIME*)

> Un temps de chien
> **A time of dog**
>
> ☞ *Bad weather*

> C'est un vrai temps de cochon
> **It's a real weather of pig**
>
> ☞ *It's a filthy weather*

TÉNÉBREUX (*GLOOMY*)

> Un beau ténébreux
> **A beautiful gloomy**
>
> ☞ *A darkly handsome man*

TENIR (TO HOLD)

Un tiens vaut mieux que deux tu l'auras
**A hold is better than two
you will hold it**

☞ *A bird in the hand is worth two
in the bush*

TÊTE (HEAD)

Faire une sale tête
To make a dirty head

☞ *To have a nasty mug*

Être la tête de Turc
To be the turkish head

☞ *To be the scapegoat*

Tête à queue
Head to tail

☞ *Slew*

Tête-bêche
Head-spade

☞ *Top to bottom*

C'est une tête de lard
He is a head of bacon

☞ *He is as stubborn as a mule*

Ça va pas la tête ?
It's not going the head ?

☞ *Are you crazy ?*

J'ai trop bu hier soir. J'ai la tête dans le cul
I drank too much last night.
I have the head in the ass

☞ *I over drunk last night. I have a hangover*

Un tête-à-tête à la belle étoile
A head to head at the nice star

☞ *A night-time tryst*

THE (THE)

Il croyait que c'était in the pocket
et il l'a eu in the baba
He thought it was in the pocket
and he got it in the baba

☞ *He thought everything was fine*
  and then he was had

256

THON (*TUNA FISH*)

Ta sœur c'est un gros thon !
Your sister is a big tuna fish !

☞ *Your sister is a dog*

TICKET (*TICKET*)

Il a un ticket d'accord, mais on dirait
Simone de Beauvoir
**He has a ticket OK, but she looks
like Simone of Nice See**

☞ *O.K, so she likes him, but she looks like
Simone de Beauvoir*

TIEN (*YOURS*)

À la tienne, Étienne
At the yours, Steve

☞ *Cheers*

TIMBRER (*TO STAMP*)

Être timbré
To be stamped

☞ *To be round the bend*

257

TIRER (*TO SHOOT*)

À tire-d'aile
At shoot-wing

☞ *Swiftly*

J'adore tirer les rois
I love to shoot the kings

☞ *I love celebrating twelfth-night*

Je me tire, j'ai rancart
à Marcadet-Poissonnière
**I shoot myself, I have an appointment
at Marcadet-Fishmonger**

☞ *I'm off ! I'm meeting someone
at Marcadet-Poissonnière*

Être tiré à quatre épingles
To be drawn at four pins

☞ *To be dressed up to the nines*

TOILE (*LINEN*)

Ce soir, je me ferais bien une toile
**Tonight, I would make me well
a linen**

☞ *I'd like to see a film this evening*

258

TÔLE (*SHEET IRON*)

> Je me suis tôlé en moto
> et à mes examens
> **I sheet ironed in motorbike**
> **and at my exams**
>
> ☞ *My motorbike crashed*
> *and I failed my exam*

TOMBER (*TO FALL*)

> Il tombe à point nommé
> **He falls at named point**
>
> ☞ *He comes just in time*

TONNEAU (*BARREL*)

> C'est du même tonneau
> **It is of the same barrel**
>
> ☞ *It is the same thing*

TORCHON (*TEATOWEL*)

> Il ne faut pas mélanger les torchons
> et les serviettes
> **Don't mix the teatowels**
> **and the napkins**
>
> ☞ *We must divide the steep from the gots*

TORDRE (*TO TWIST*)

>Un tord-boyaux
>**A twist bowels**
>
>☞ *A hot gut*

TOUR (*TOWER*)

>À double tour
>**At double tower**
>
>☞ *To double lock*
>
>Faire un tour de cochon
>**To make a tower of pig**
>
>☞ *To trick*
>
>En un tour de main
>**On one tower of hand**
>
>☞ *In a flash*
>
>Le tour est joué
>**The tower is played**
>
>☞ *The trick has worked*

TOURNER (TO TURN)

Être mal tourné
To be badly turned

☞ To be in a bad mood

Ça tourne en eau de boudin
It turns into water of sausage

☞ It dies on the vine

TOUT (ALL)

Touche-à-tout
Touch-to-all

☞ To have a finger in every pie

Jouer le tout pour le tout
To play the all for the all

☞ To risk everything

Le Tout-Paris
The all-Paris

☞ The smart set

À tout'
At all

☞ See you later

261

TRACER (TO TRACE)

> J'me trace, j'rentre à Juvisy-sur-Orge
> **I am tracing myself, I go back
> to Juvisy on Barley**
>
> ☞ *I'm leaving, I'm going back
> to Juvisy-sur-Orge*

TRADUIRE (TO TRANSLATE)

> Traduire quelqu'un en justice
> **To translate somebody in Court**
>
> ☞ *To prosecute*

TRAIN (TRAIN)

> Se magner le train
> **To move one's train**
>
> ☞ *To hurry up*
>
> Filer le train
> **To spin the train**
>
> ☞ *To follow*

TRANCHE (SLICE)

J'en ai rien à secouer de cette tranche
de cake
**I have nothing to shake of this slice
of cake**

☞ *I've nothing to do with that fool*

S'en payer une tranche
To pay one's slice

☞ *To have goodtime*

TRANQUILLE (QUIET)

Tranquille comme Baptiste
Quiet like Baptiste

☞ *Very quiet*

TRANSI (CHILLED)

Un amoureux transi
A chilled lover

☞ *A bashful lover*

TRAVAIL (WORK)

Et voilà le travail
And here is the work

☞ Here we are ! It's finished

TRAVAILLER (TO WORK)

Travailler du chapeau
To work from the hat

☞ To be crazy

TRENTE ET UN (THIRTY ONE)

Se mettre sur son trente et un
To put oneself on one's thirty one

☞ To dress up

Être sur son trente-et-un
To be on one's thirty one

☞ To dress up

TRIP (TRIP)

J'suis allé à une soirée ; j'ai bien tripé
**I went to a party where
I well tripped**

☞ I went to a party and had a fun time

Elle fait le trottoir
(She is a street walker)

TROMBONE (*PAPER CLIP*)

Il joue du trombone dans la salle
des pas perdus
**He is playing paper clip in the room
of the lost foot steps**

☞ *He is playing the trombone
in the booking hall*

TRONC (*TRUNK*)

Je ne veux plus me casser le tronc
pour toi
**I don't want to break me the trunk
for you**

☞ *I don't want to put myself out for you*

TROP (*TOO MUCH*)

Ce mec est trop
This guy is too much

☞ *What a lovely guy*

TROTTOIR (*PAVEMENT*)

Elle fait le trottoir
She is making the pavement

☞ *She is a street walker*

TROU (HOLE)

Boire comme un trou
To drink like a hole

☞ *To drink a lot*

TRUAND (CROOK)

Si ça se trouve, tu t'es fait truander
If it finds you make yourself crooked

☞ *It may be that you were conned*

TU (YOU)

Être à tu et à toi
To be at you and at you

☞ *To be on firstname basis*

TUBE (TUBE)

Je me suis fait entuber de dix sacs
I made myself intubed of ten bags

☞ *I was robbed of hundred francs*

U, V

Un (ONE)

Il était moins une
It was less one

☞ *It was a narrow escape*

Cinq colonnes à la une
Five columns at the one

☞ *Front page*

Vache (COW)

C'est vachement chouette
It is cowly owl

☞ *It is very nice*

Quelle peau de vache !
What a skin of cow !

☞ *Bastard !*

Il parle français comme une vache
espagnole
**He speaks French like
a Spanish cow**

☞ *He absolutely murders
the French language*

271

Ah la vache !
Ah the cow !

☞ *Wow !*

Il habite sur le plateau de Millevaches
**He lives on the tray
of One Thousand Cows**

☞ *He lives on the plateau de Millevaches*

J'ai besoin du plancher des vaches
I need the floor of the cows

☞ *I need dry land*

VAGUE (*WAVE*)

Avoir du vague à l'âme
To have wave to soul

☞ *To be unsettled*

VALISE (*SUITCASE*)

Se faire la valise
To make oneself the suitcase

☞ *To leave*

Il a des valises sous les yeux
He gets suitcases under the eyes

☞ *He has bags under his eyes*

Il a des valises sous les yeux
(*He has bags under his eyes*)

Bordel à queue ! T'es con comme
une valise
**Bordello at tail ! You are as stupid
as a suitcase**

☞ *Christ ! You are so dumb !*

VANNE (*SLUICE*)

Faut pas charrier, j'étais juste
en train de te vanner
**Do not carry, I was just in train
to sluice yourself**

☞ *Don't get mad I was only teasing !*

VASE (*MUD*)

Être vaseux
To be muddy

☞ *To be washed out*

VEINE (*VEIN*)

Avoir une veine de pendu
To have a vein of hanged

☞ *To be very lucky*

VÉLO (BICYCLE)

Je crois qu'il a un petit vélo
I think he has a little bicycle

☞ *I think he has bats in the belfry*

VELOURS (VELVET)

Il joue sur du velours
He is playing on velvet

☞ *He is onto a sure thing*

VENIR (TO COME)

Viens chez moi, j'habite chez une copine
**Come at my place, I live
at a girlfriend's place**

☞ *Come to my place, I live
at my girlfriend's*

VER (WORM)

Ne pas être piqué des vers
Not to be picked by the worms

☞ *To be first rate*

275

VERNIS (*VARNISH*)

>Être verni
>**To be varnished**
>
>☞ *To be lucky*

VÉROLE (*POX*)

>Comme la vérole sur le bas clergé breton
>**Like pox on the Breton low clergy**
>
>☞ *Like a bat out of hell*

VERRE (*GLASS*)

>Il a un verre dans le nez
>**He has a glass in the nose**
>
>☞ *He has had one too many*

VERT (*GREEN*)

>Raconter des vertes et des pas mûres
>**To tell green and not ripe**
>
>☞ *To tell spicy*

VESSIE (*BLADDER*)

Il prend les vessies pour des lanternes
He is taking bladders for lanterns

☞ *He would have us believe that the moon is made of green cheese*

VESTE (*JACKET*)

Ramasser une veste
To pick up a jacket

☞ *To fail*

Il a retourné sa veste
He reversed his jacket

☞ *He changed his time*

VEXÉ (*UPSET*)

Il est vexé comme un pou
He is upset like a louse

☞ *He is really livid*

VIDER (*TO EMPTY*)

Je lui ai vidé mon sac
I emptied my bag

☞ *I came out with it*

VIE (*LIFE*)

Une vie de bâton de chaise
A life of stick of chair

☞ *A rollicking life*

VIEUX (*OLD*)

Un vieux de la vieille
An old of the old

☞ *A very old person*

Un vieux beau
An old nice

☞ *An old don Juan*

VIN (*WINE*)

Je suis sûr qu'il reçoit des pots de vin
I am sure he gets pots of wine

☞ *I am sure he gets bribes*

Avoir le vin triste
To have the sad wine

☞ *To be a sad drunk*

Être entre deux vins
To be between two wines

☞ *To be half sober*

VINGT (*TWENTY*)

Vingt-deux, voilà les keufs !
Twenty two, here are the cops !

☞ *Watch out ! Here come the cops !*

VIOLON (*VIOLIN*)

Ça ou pisser dans un violon !
This or pissing in a violin !

☞ *This, or water off a duck's back !*

J'ai passé la nuit au violon
I spent the night at the violin

☞ *I spent the night in the nick*

VIVRE (*TO LIVE*)

Être sur le qui-vive
To be on the who-lives

☞ *To be on the alert*

VOILE (*SAIL*)

> J'en connais un qui est à voile et à vapeur
> **I know one who is at sail and steam**
>
> ☞ *I know someone who swings both ways*

> Toutes voiles dehors
> **All sails out**
>
> ☞ *Under full sail*

VOIR (*TO SEE*)

> Un m'as-tu vu
> **A have you seen me**
>
> ☞ *A conceited person*

VOITURE (*CAR*)

> En voiture Simone !
> **In the car Simone !**
>
> ☞ *Go ahead !*

VOIX (*VOICE*)

> Avoir voix au chapitre
> **To have voice to the chapter**
>
> ☞ *To have a say in the matter*

280

VOL (*ROBERRY*)

> Faire du vol à voile
> **To do sailing robbery**
>
> ☞ *To glide*

VOLER (*TO STEAL*)

> Qui vole un œuf vole un bœuf
> **Who steals an egg steals an ox**
>
> ☞ *Who steals a penny steals a pound*

VOLET (*SHUTTER*)

> Ils étaient triés sur le volet
> **They were sorted on the shutter**
>
> ☞ *They were hand picked*

VÔTRE (*YOURS*)

> À la bonne vôtre
> **At the good yours**
>
> ☞ *Your health*

VOULOIR (TO WANT)

En veux-tu, en voilà
Do you want some, here there are

☞ *As many as you want*

VOYAGE (TRAVEL)

J'ai pas été déçu du voyage
**I was not disappointed
with the travel**

☞ *That was quite something*

VUE (SIGHT)

À vue de nez
At sight of nose

☞ *At a rough estimate*

W, X,
Y, Z

Un wagon-lit
(*A sleeping car*)

WAGON (*WAGON*)

> Un wagon-lit
> **A bed-wagon**
>
> ☞ *A sleeping car*

X (*X*)

> Il a fait l'X
> **He made the X**
>
> ☞ *He studied at the Polytechnic Institute*

ZÈBRE (*ZEBRA*)

> Un drôle de zèbre
> **A funny zebra**
>
> ☞ *A peculiar person*

ZÉRO (*ZERO*)

> Les avoir à zéro
> **To have them at zero**
>
> ☞ *To be frightened*

ZONE (ZONE)

Chez toi c'est vraiment la zone
At your place it is really the zone

☞ *Your place is a pigsty*

ZOUAVE (MAN OF THE ALMA BRIDGE)

Faire le zouave
To make the man of the Alma bridge

☞ *To brag*

Un drôle de zèbre
(A peculiar person)

La Théière de Chardin : jeux de noms
(en collaboration avec Gilbert de Goy, illustrations de Clab)
Garnier, 1979

Agenda du V.I.P. (Very Important Person)
Garnier, 1981

Almaniaque de la France profonde
AMP Éditions, 1982

La Khomenie du pouvoir
Scorpio, 1982

Mon carnet secret F.M.
(illustrations de Michel Boucher)
Carrère, 1986

FDG, Le Guide du Futur Directeur Général
(en collaboration avec Marie Garagnoux, illustrations de Yan Nascimbene)
Hermé, 1986

Culture + : un livre-jeu pour tester vos connaissances
(en collaboration avec Marie Garagnoux et Patrick Michel Dansac)
Carrère, 1987

**Les Meilleures Histoires de bonnes manières
et autres préceptes auxquels vous avez échappé !**
Carrère, 1987

Sky ! my teacher : cours d'anglais très particulier
(illustrations de Clab)
Carrère, 1987, 1988

Culture + : préparez le bac en jouant
(en collaboration avec Marie Garagnoux et Patrick Michel Dansac)
Carrère, 1988

Almanach Hachette 1989
Hachette Pratique, 1988

Heaume sweet home
Dictionnaire illustré des homonymes franco-anglais
Harrap, 1989

Almanach Hachette 1990
Hachette Pratique, 1989

L'Agenda du Jet set
Le Cherche-Midi, 1990

Almanach Hachette 1991
Hachette Pratique, 1990

Édouard, ça m'interpelle !
Le français nouveau est arrivé
(en collaboration avec Pascale Leroy)
Belfond, 1991

Le Dictionnaire des mots qui n'existent pas
(en collaboration avec Nathalie Kristy,
illustrations de Gilles Bachelet)
Hors Collection, 1992
et « Pocket », n° 4305

Un si gentil petit garçon
mémoires
Payot, 1992
et « Points », n° P1912

L'Anglais saugrenu
(illustrations de Christine Géricot)
Payot, 1993
et « Points », n° P20
édition revue et augmentée sous le titre

Guide farfelu mais nécessaire
de conversation anglaise
Points, « Le Goût des mots », n° P2603, 2011

Sky Mr. Allgood ! Parlons français avec M. Toubon
Mille et Une Nuits, 1994

Ad aeroportum! (À l'aéroport!) : le latin d'aujourd'hui
Mots & Cie, 1999

Le Cafard laqué : les mots-portemanteaux
Mots & Cie, 1999

Nouilles ou pâtes?
Le bon sens des mots
Mots & Cie, 1999

Mes perles de culture : un catalogue déraisonne
Mots & Cie, 2000

Wit spirit vol. 1 : L'humour anglo-saxon
Mots & Cie, 2000

L'Almanach Chiflet 2001
Mots & Cie, 2000

Ciel! Blake : dictionnaire français-anglais
des expressions courantes
Sky! Mortimer : English-French dictionary
of running idioms
Mots & Cie, 2000

Wit spirit vol. 2 : L'humour anglo-saxon
Mots & Cie, 2001

Roger au pays des mots
(illustrations de Cabu)
Mots & Cie, 2001

On ne badine pas avec l'humour :
de l'humour et de sa nécessité
(en collaboration avec Maryz Courberand)
Mots & Cie, 2001

Schtroumpfez-vous français : les schtroumpferies
de la langue française
Mots & Cie, 2002

Antigone de la nouille
Mots & Cie, 2002

J'ai un mot à vous dire : un mot se raconte...
Mots & Cie, 2002

Réflexions faites... et autres libres pensées
Mots & Cie, 2003

Le Mokimanké : le dico des mots qui existent enfin !
(avec Nathalie Kristy)
Mots & Cie, 2003

Malheur au bonheur !
Le guide du sous-développement personnel
Mots & Cie, 2004

Nom d'une pipe ! : dictionnaire français-anglais
des expressions courantes (2)
Name of a pipe ! : English-French dictionary
of running idioms (2)
Mots & Cie, 2004

Petit dictionnaire des mots retrouvés
(préface de Jean d'Ormesson)
Mots & Cie, 2004

L'Agenda du V.I.P.
Mots & Cie, 2004

Le Diconoclaste : dictionnaire espiègle et saugrenu
Chiflet & Cie, 2005

Loftum Vaticanum : le vade-mecum du conclave
(en collaboration avec Lise Fitaire et Anne Camberlin)
Chiflet & Cie, 2005

So irresistible ! Deux siècles d'humour anglo-saxon
Chiflet & Cie, 2005
et « J'ai lu », n° 8242

So incredible ! Toujours plus d'humour anglo-saxon
Chiflet & Cie, 2006

The New Yorker : les meilleurs dessins
sur la France et les Français
Éditions des Arènes, 2006
et nouvelle édition sous le titre
La France et les Français
200 dessins
« Points », n° P2522

Le Coup de Chiflet
Chiflet & Cie, 2006

Les mots qui me font rire
et autres cocasseries de la langue française
Points, « Le Goût des mots », 2007

The New Yorker, les dessins inédits
Éditions des Arènes, 2007

Comment résister aux fêtes de fin d'année
Chiflet & Cie, 2007

... Suites et fins
Chiflet & Cie, 2008

SPorc ou cochon : les faux-semblants
Chiflet & Cie, 2009

Un éclat de rire par jour
Calendrier 2010
Hugo Image, 2009

99 mots et expressions à foutre à la poubelle
(illustrations de Pascal Le Brun)
Points, « Le Goût des mots », n° P2268, 2009

J'ai encore un mot à vous dire
Chiflet & Cie, 2010

99 clichés à foutre à la poubelle
(illustrations de Pascal Le Brun)
Points, « Le Goût des mots », n° P2503, 2010

RÉALISATION : NORD COMPO MULTIMÉDIA
À VILLENEUVE D'ASCQ
IMPRESSION : CPI FIRMIN DIDOT, À MESNIL-SUR-L'ESTRÉE
DÉPÔT LÉGAL : NOVEMBRE 2008. N° 98547-6 (104243)
IMPRIMÉ EN FRANCE